Apples From My Orchard

Prose and Poetry

Doris,

Thank you

Be well

Enjoy

Yohoghua

Apples From My Orchard

Prose and Poetry

Yehoshua Karsh

iUniverse, Inc.
New York Bloomington

Apples From My Orchard
Prose and Poetry

iUniverse books may be ordered through booksellers or by contacting:

iUniverse
1663 Liberty Drive
Bloomington, IN 47403
www.iuniverse.com
1-800-Authors (1-800-288-4677)

Because of the dynamic nature of the Internet, any Web addresses or links contained in this book may have changed since publication and may no longer be valid. The views expressed in this work are solely those of the author and do not necessarily reflect the views of the publisher, and the publisher hereby disclaims any responsibility for them.

ISBN: 978-1-4401-5701-1 (pbk)
ISBN: 978-1-4401-5702-8 (dj)
ISBN: 978-1-4401-5703-5 (ebk)

Printed in the United States of America

iUniverse rev. date: 8/04/2009

I dedicate this volume to my dear friends, Fred and Marla Lappe. They have been so important, in so many ways, to my family and me, and we are better people because of it. I can never repay their selfless giving; the best I can do is try to emulate them.

For my mother (and editor), her love of teaching and the written word have been an inspiration to me for as long as I can remember.

Contents

Prose

Prose

Silence is Torah Too

My teacher, Rabbi Moshe Shapiro shlita, was once teaching us. One of the students placed a small tape recorder on the table in front of him to record the class. Rav Moshe noticed that the tape recorder made a slight click whenever he was silent and asked the student why it did that. The student explained that the tape recorder was sensitive to sound and would pause from recording when there was silence. Rav Moshe paused for a moment, and then said that was too bad, because the silence was also Torah.

My Screen-Saver Mode

I have a mode of functioning I call 'screen-saver' mode. This is not just one of my modes of functioning, it is the status quo. I use just enough energy to keep a dim light of awareness going, but there's not much else happening 'under the hood.'

Every once in a while I wake up. I notice something; it could be the sound of birds chirping, the smell of spring, a beautiful quality in someone I've known for a long time, or a palpable sense of G-d's presence. The moment lasts for only a short while, and then I'm back to 'screen-saver.'

The Torah knows about my 'screen-saver' mode and designed mitzvot to wake me out of it. When I make a blessing, wear tzitzit, or stop to take notice of the message in the mezuzah, I am called to attention, like moving a *mouse* recalls the computer to full functionality.

If I could only remain aware; there are so many things I've thought about doing or changing but never got around to because after a moment or two ... click, the 'screen-saver' came back on.

Just Go in the Way of G-d

I know it's serious, and vitally important, but when you first read it, it's hilarious. I'm talking about the line in the Torah that reads:

"Now Israel, what does Hashem your G-d ask of you, but to be in awe of Hashem your G-d, to go in all of His ways; and to love Him and to serve Him with all of your heart and all of your soul. (Devarim, 10/12)"

It seems like the Torah is suggesting that being what Hashem wants us to be is not that difficult. All you have to do is .... But when you read the fine print, what we are being asked to do, besides being in awe of and loving G-d, is to follow in *all of his ways*, and to do it all with every fiber of our being. That is a mountain, not just a mountain; it is the Mount Everest of expectations. And it all begins with something like: "*What is He really asking of you, not much, just a little....everything you can imagine, done in the best way possible!!*" That is funny!

Then when the laughter dies down; and we wipe the tears from our eyes, we understand that there couldn't be a more important message for the well meaning members of our generation:

We begin to feel it in high school, but it continues for decades. We have this sense that we have to become something, that we have to fulfill some mysterious potential; and only when we do that, will our life really be a success. Somehow, this mysterious achievement will be related to our professional life; and everything, I mean everything, hangs on whether we discover what that mysterious vocation is and that we achieve greatness in it. The anxiety that comes of this belief makes up part of the background noise of our lives. It's like we were born into a Kafka story, into some mystery that everyone else understands, but us. What am I supposed to be <u>doing</u>? Is this my life's work? Am I a success? Will I be a success?

I have a friend who is a musical genius. As a child he was a prodigy, and ever since then he has made a living playing and arranging Jewish music. He freely admits that the music is simple and not very creative, but it pays the bills. For years friends and admirers would pester him to do more with his talent. To develop his abilities further, to do something truly, musically, special. One day he went to visit the Steipler Z"L and asked him if he was required to make something special of his talent. The Steipler said; "Talent is like a towel, if your hands are wet, you wipe them on the towel." He understood that to mean: You only have to do something with your talent if you feel the need to.

3

It took me a long time to understand what the Steipler meant, but I think I get it now. He meant what our teaching from the Torah means: You don't have to become something mysterious, do something yet unknown but spectacular, to fulfill G-d's plan for you. All you have to do is be in awe..... Which admittedly is a lot, but it is not mysterious. Your life is not a Kafka story, there is no need for existential anxiety, just do what is in front of you, and do it as well as you can. After all, that is how you climb a mountain; you pay attention and set one foot down in front of the other. Oh, and you get a good Sherpa.

The Perfect Book

I imagine that one day I will meet someone and introduce myself to him and he will be very excited. He will say; "So you're Yehoshua Karsh. You wrote the most wonderful book." And I'll be very proud and excited that my book was received with such favor. And then he'll go on to tell me that he and some friends have formed a club that meets regularly, and all of them agree that my book is perfect.

My elation will know no bounds not only does this man like my book, his friends think its perfect. Then my newly discovered fan will go on to explain that he and his friends are collectors, they collect paperweights, and each of them has an extensive collection. Whenever they meet, they compare each other's collections and eventually get to discuss the various qualities that would make up the perfect paperweight. They agree on what most of those qualities would be and the moment they saw my book, they recognized every one of those qualities in it. It was … the perfect paperweight.

He will then pause nervously and ask if I would mind visiting his club. They would all be thrilled to meet me. It will take me a moment to recover from the shock of hearing that my book is revered not because of its content, but because of its paperweight qualities; and then I will smile and tell myself that as long as it is appreciated, I shouldn't care why. And with satisfaction, I will turn to the man, and tell him that I would love to visit with his club.

Facing G-d

"Shiviti Hashem L'Negdi Tamid…(Tehilim/Psalms 16:8)"
Translation: "I have set G-d before me always…"

Rabbi Moshe Isserlish begins his comments on the Shulchan Aruch (Code of Jewish Law) with this phrase. It is often found on the podium from which the Chazzan leads the prayers. I always thought it meant that I should remember that G-d is before me, but lately I've decided that it doesn't mean that at all.

If you pay attention to the wording, it is actually a very arrogant statement. I speak as if it is I who place G-d before me, as if He is some object which is moved from place to place for my benefit.

In English there is a phrase: "Put the wind to your back." Obviously the wind is not something you can just put somewhere. The phrase means; turn yourself so that the wind is at your back. The same is true with the statement from Tehilim. It means; turn your self towards G-d, face Him. I may not be able to see his face, but I must show him mine.

What Were They Thinking?

Several years ago I visited Grants Farm in St. Louis and together with my family watched the elephants perform. At one point during the show a presenter pointed out that the elephant is a Pachyderm. Pachyderm means thick skin. I don't know why it struck me just then, but I was overcome with laughter; of all the things to identify as the unique characteristic of an elephant. I mean, what about its size? How about the tusks? The ears... they're huge! But no, the elephant will forever be identified as ... 'thick skinned.'

Some time later I had a similar experience when reading about Petra in Jordan. Petra is considered one of the geological wonders of the world. The gorgeous colors of the stone and the unique formations of the rock have made it one of the great tourist spots of the Middle East. One day, it just struck me; Petra means rock in Latin. All of that beauty, majesty, and wonder; and the best they could do was; 'Rock.' That's like naming the Grand Canyon, 'Hole' or Mount Everest, 'Mound.'

It was in a similar vein that I was struck, not long ago, with the curious naming of mankind. The Torah calls us Adam, because we came from the Adama (earth). Assuming that the value of our name is that it distinguishes us from the things around us, that it identifies a feature that is unique to us, the last thing we should be called is Adam. Everything on earth is of the earth. Call us Neshama (soul), or Medaber (speaker) or Yodeah (sapian), or something else that distinguishes us from the rest of creation.

Maybe we're called Adam for us, not to help other creatures identify us. After all, they don't use words or class distinctions; that is something we do. Maybe we need to be reminded that while we have so many unique and wonderful qualities, we are still of the earth. We have humble beginnings and endings, and shouldn't get too carried away with ourselves. Maybe we also need to remember that we don't just interact with the environment, we are the environment. We don't just live on the earth, we are the earth.

I shared the above with my brother in-law Larry, and he made the following observations:

Perhaps they named the elephant pachyderm because initially elephants were used as armored war vehicles. It was their thick skin that made them so invulnerable to the arrows and spears of their enemy and thus useful.

Petra is named rock because of an ancient Arab tradition that it is the site of the spot where Moshe struck 'the rock,' in order to produce water.

Mercifully he came to the same conclusion I did about the naming of mankind.

Falling Acorns

At the end of summer, the oak trees in my neighborhood, and I assume, in every neighborhood, drop their acorns. They are everywhere. The tires of my car crunch many, the grass is dotted with them; sometimes I hear the click and pop of them landing on the sidewalk. It seems a waste to me, there are so many acorns, yet so few of them will ever become a tree!

In a similar vein, it once occurred to me that the manner in which Judaism is continued is highly inefficient. All those born of a Jewish mother are Jewish. According to the Torah, they are bound to the covenants of Avraham and Sinai, whether they want to be or not. In every generation there are many who choose not to follow the statutes set down in the covenants; according to the Torah, they and the entire Jewish people are judged unfavorably because of that. It has happened, in every generation since the beginning of the Jewish people, that Jews have tried to opt out of the mission of the Jewish people, but according to the Torah, they cannot.

Wouldn't it have been more efficient to design the system so that only those who wanted to be a part of the mission were a part of the mission, a voluntary army, instead a "draft"? That way we could be a "light unto the nations" without any confusion; we would look like G-d wanted us to look, because everyone called a Jew would be devoted to playing the role G-d set forth. But it's not that way, we are not a voluntary membership.

Then an idea suggested itself. Maybe biological continuity is the best of all scenarios. Maybe we need a certain number of dropouts to challenge us, to criticize us, to force us to be better, to teach, and to give to. If we were just a bunch of people who agreed about everything, we would become arrogant, narrow minded, and corrupt; and never know it. Now, I might be all of those things, but there is no end to the people who are willing to let me know about it.

Dying (A Metaphoric Exploration of Mortality)

I am dying.

I am sorry to burden you with my plight, but I need to share this with someone. You needn't respond; just having someone listen to me greatly relieves the burden of my terrible knowledge.

Let me begin by asserting that I want nothing more than to live. (If this weren't about something as grave as my own death, I might laugh at that last statement because, while I mean every word of that assertion, I actually go about the process of living without great fervor. I rarely spend my time engaged in meaningful activity. I am often bored. Yet there is nothing so frightening to me as my death; and as I told you, I have just discovered that I am to die.)

My first thought when I discovered that I was to die was, could there be anything more ridiculous? This disease which grasps on to me is a parasite living off of my life force until it uses up the very energy it needs to survive. Foolish disease, don't you realize that by using up my life force you deny yourself the very energy you need to continue to survive? If we could just come to some agreement, you would continue to draw of my life force, but just what you need to survive, and leave me the rest. Then we could both continue and no one would be the worse for it. But you are greedy, you want more and more and eventually your unabated lust will be the end of us both. Foolish, foolish, disease.

You might wonder how it is that I am going to die when you and I both know that the creation is renewed every second. Whatever disease or malady I might possess should certainly not survive into the next moment of creation, when everything comes out of nothing and is completely refreshed and renewed. And yet it does, and do you know why? I am embarrassed to tell you why, but I will tell you just the same. The reason my disease survives into the next, the newest and freshest moment of creation, is because ... I hold on to it. You thought that it was the disease that was holding on to me, but that is only an illusion. It is I who refuse to let go of my disease, even for a moment. It would disappear in an instant, into the past, if I just released my hold on it, but I refuse, I won't let it go. I, who fear death more than anything, hold on to my disease and keep it alive. I give it sustenance. I carefully make room for it in every new 'world' that comes. Can you imagine anything more foolish?

Do you know why I hold on to my disease, even though I know it will bring about my own end? I do it because I want to have something. I want something that is my own, something I don't have to ask permission to use; something I don't have to share with anyone, not even Hashem. I want to keep it in a treasure box and take it out to play with or just to look at whenever I feel the need.

I see you know where my mistake lies. It is that I have replaced 'becoming' with owning. It is so much easier to have something than to be something. And with some effort, on some occasions, I have even convinced myself that if I 'have' something, I 'am' something.

Yes, I know, I know, if I would just focus on 'being' instead of 'owning' I would live forever. But it takes so much effort and I am weary, you see ... I am dying.

Teaching the Akeidah

Roneen brought up a question her daughter asked, when we discussed the 'Binding of Isaac:'

"If G-d asked you to kill me, would you do it?"

Roneen asked what we would answer if asked that question by our children. I loved the question and asked friends and colleagues how they would respond. And I continue to solicit responses to this day.

The best response I've had so far was given by Jack, a tough on the outside, sweet on the inside, member of a class at Crestview Capitol. Jack was late to class that day, arriving after I had asked Roneen's question, and there had already been a bit of discussion about it by the time he arrived. Stewart, one of the class members, asked Jack what he would tell his kids, and Jack, said: "I'd tell him that if G-d asked me to kill you, I'd do it. What can I say? It's the truth."

Then Stewart asked him: "What if it was your Grandchild?"

Without a pause, Jack said:

"No, that I'd never do."

The Test

A few years ago, I day-dreamed the basic components of the following scene:

I was a contestant on a Game Show. The theme of the show was testing your faith. I was asked, by the host, whether I believed that the description of the giving of the Torah at Sinai was true as it was presented in the Torah. I immediately answered yes. He smiled, held out an envelope, and proceeded to tell me that in the envelope was incontrovertible proof as to whether the account of The Giving of the Torah, as presented in the Torah, was factually correct. He assured me that, upon seeing the proof, I would agree that it proved the issue one way or another; and that if I didn't accept the proof in the end, I could be assured that all bets would be off. I agreed to go on. He then challenged me to a wager. But before we actually wagered, he asked if I would agree to have an emotion detector attached to me, so that my state of calm could be measured during the challenge. There would be three categories of measured response: normal, anxious, and panic. I agree to be monitored.

The first wager was ten dollars. Would I wager ten dollars that the account of The Giving of the Torah was true? I said yes, and the emotion detector showed not even the slightest indication of concern. Next he asked if I would wager a hundred dollars. Again I said yes, and again there was no indication of change. He then moved on to a thousand, and again there was no change. Now he asked if I would wager all of my earthly belongings. I paused, swallowed, and answered yes. The emotion detector registered anxious. At that point, the host directed my attention to a curtain which slowly opened to show my family, suspended in a net, over a pool of hungry piranhas. The host now asked if I would wager my family. I would receive a new car if the account was true, and if not my family would be released into the pool of piranhas. He then added, with a sinister smile, that for a man of faith it should be an easy wager. The monitor registered panic.

End of day-dream.

I learned at that moment that belief/faith is not a place you arrive at, but a continuum. There is no point of faith that, once arrived at, qualifies me as a person of faith. I can have faith at one level, but be challenged at the next. My goal is to move as far along the continuum as I can; so that as each new challenge arrives, I can meet it with faith.

Stream of Consciousness

Today I was studying about prophecy with Mayer when he wondered out loud how a prophet can identify that a particular event he sees will happen in the future; after all, the information that he is accessing is most likely coming from a "place" beyond the boundaries of time.

His question began a stream of consciousness that led me to remember a question that occurred to me a few months ago. Can a gilgul (reincarnated soul) go back in time? When your soul leaves your body, it is most likely beyond the boundaries of time. If that is so, and it decides to come back in order to fix something it did or do something it left undone, why do we assume it will come back during a time that is further along the linear timeline from its death? And if it can go back in time, some of the people we are in contact with could have souls from the future. My soul may be from the future.

This thought led me to think: What do I mean when I say 'my soul?' Who is this 'I' that possesses the soul? Aren't I my soul?

This led me to think that my relationship with my past is the closest I will come to experiencing death. Every moment is a new reality. The moment before is no longer accessible, it is static, done, as I imagine my life will look to me after I die.

This then led me to think that nothing is really static. Although a table appears solid and static to me, it is really made up of atoms which are themselves made up of nuclei that have electrons whizzing around them. Glass is a liquid and is flowing in super slow motion. Even my past only has the appearance of permanence. It is changing based on the continuing effects of those past actions and can change if I repent wrongs committed.

This led me to think that the soles on my shoes are wearing thin, and I really need to buy a new pair.

This led me to think that I haven't had a good pear in a long while.

This led me to get hungry.

This led me to get up and look in the fridge for something to eat.

When I got there, I couldn't remember what I was looking for.

Rav Moshe and the Watch

Several years ago Hillel asked Rav Moshe Shapiro Shlita a question:

Hillel had a friend who learned at BMT, in a program designed by Rav Subato. The members of this program learned all of Talmud in one year. If a person learned one page (in Talmud one page means two sides of text) of Talmud a day, it would take him over seven years to finish it, and these students were learning it in one year. They weren't just reading it, they were learning it. They had systems for review and study, which took their every waking moment, every day of the year, including Shabbos and Holidays.

Hillel asked Rav Moshe if that wasn't the best way to go about things. First you immerse yourself in the general body of information, and then you go back and study the subjects in depth. That way, you had the entire corpus of Talmud as reference whenever you were trying to unravel the depths of meaning of a particular piece of Talmud.

By the time Hillel finished asking his question, a crowd of students had gathered to hear Rav Moshe's response. He pointed to one of the students, Menachem, and asked him to give him his watch. Rav Moshe said that he was going to ask Menachem, several questions about the appearance of his watch. These would be questions like: "Is there a second hand?" or "What is the color of the face of your watch?" Not about minutia, but about things that would be obvious to any observer. Rav Moshe had picked the right person for this exercise. He knew that Menachem had little concern for the details of something like a watch, and that was Rav Moshe's point. Before he asked about the watch itself, he asked Menachem how many times he had looked at the watch. Menachem guessed ten thousand. Rav Moshe then proceeded to ask Menachem ten questions about his watch and Menachem answered every one of them incorrectly.

Rav Moshe then made his point: How can it be that a highly intelligent person, can look at something ten thousand times, and not know obvious facts about it? The answer is, he doesn't care. He never took time to observe the watch for its own sake it was just for telling time. If you don't take the time to learn something for its own sake, but rather because you have some other purpose in mind, you will not learn the thing in the first place. If you study Talmud because you want to finish it, not because you are interested in a particular discussion, you will not remember a thing. The best method for studying Talmud is to approach each discussion and make it your focus. Learn it for its own sake, care about the outcome, and then you will know it.

According to Nacmanides, the purpose of revealed miracles is to open our eyes to the reality that everything is in fact miraculously maintained by G-d. But why don't we see that always, why do we need miracles to show us what is always before our eyes? Perhaps it's as simple as: we don't care to look. If so, then all we need to see the Hand of G-d miraculously revealed in creation, is to pay attention

Derech Eretz

Sometimes I am reminded that basically good, healthy, people, can do horrible things. I am also reminded that if you don't start off as a basically good person, no amount of Torah is going to help you. That is one of the lessons the sages are teaching when they say:

"Derech Eretz Kadma L'Torah." Translation: "Good Character comes before Torah."

This is why the Torah doesn't spend a lot of time preaching about honesty or the evils of anger or the advantages of forgiveness. The Torah takes for granted that the reader is of good character. But good character isn't the goal; it's the starting point. Its what you do with that character that interests the Torah.

This means, that if at the end of your life, all you can say for yourself is that you are a good person, you aren't saying very much.

I am a Projector

I am a projector. You and everything else in the world are the screens upon which I project myself. Imagine that you are with a friend, about to watch a movie on a screen, and that friend has never watched a movie before. He doesn"t know how they work. Before the movie is projected on the screen, there is just the light from the projector and the shadow of a fly on the screen. Your friend stands up and walks over to the screen and tries to shoo it away, but the fly doesn't move. He doesn't know that the fly isn't there on the screen it's on the lens of the projector.

It's the same with me. I see something in you I don't like, some imperfection and I react to it as if it is really you, but it isn't, its just a shadow of something inside of me, something crawling on the lens of my projector.

Ice Cream

How do you eat ice cream? When my son Shauli was younger he liked his in a cup, and he chose his ice cream by color, not flavor. I choose my ice cream for flavor and have always found the 'color choosers' to be curious.

When I first went to Israel to study (30 years ago; can that be, 30 years?), I was struck by how the ice cream was identified by color. You did not order pistachio or vanilla, you ordered green or white. That has since changed.

One day in particular I remember stopping with Shauli for some ice cream at the Baskin Robins in downtown Northbrook. We were driving home from school on a crisp and sunny, almost autumn, day; and it just seemed the right thing to do. He ordered a brightly colored, sherbet swirl something or other. The Baskin Robins in Northbrook is across from a park and part of a small downtown area that is meant to look like something you would find in a 1950's TV show. There is a bike shop, an ice cream store, a library, and a small park with a baseball diamond.

Shauli and I walked over to a picnic bench in the park and went to work on our ice creams. The sun was about an hour from setting. There was a light, cool, breeze. We sat in shade provided by several tall oak trees which were busy shedding their acorns, which in turn were gathered by squirrels that seemed unconcerned about our presence.

Shauli had two trying habits when it came to eating his ice cream. The first was that after he had gone to the trouble of choosing a multi colored swirl of sherbet, he insisted on mixing it with his spoon until it ended up a raspberryish blob. And second; he ate very slowly and methodically. He would take a scoop and then lick it off in layers. I do not exaggerate when I say that he could lick one spoon load of ice cream ten or more times before it has disappeared. I have never, to my knowledge, spent more than three licks to clean my spoon. While we were both eating, his mindful licking was not a big deal; but once my Ice cream was gone, it became maddening. I tried to make conversation, but found myself watching him lick at the spoon and continuously asking: "What did you say? I'm sorry I was distracted."

I remember reading that Clarence Darrow once stuck a long pin in his cigar and proceeded to smoke it during the closing arguments of his opponent. As the ash on his cigar grew, it began to draw the attention of the jurors, and when it became impossibly long they were so enthralled, they stopped paying attention to the prosecutor entirely and Darrow won the case. Watching Shauli eat ice cream one could understand their predicament.

Sitting in the park eating ice cream with Shauli was a magical moment. I knew it would be, and it lived up to its potential. It was mostly magical because I shared it with Shauli, but the ice cream had something to do with it.

What is it about ice cream that is so wonderful? Sometimes I think about what I would do if I couldn't teach, and lately I have been thinking about serving ice cream. Have you ever seen someone take the first lick and not smile? It's a powerful thing, something that can bring a smile to everyone, good or bad, every color, race, political affiliation. Is there anything like it?

Weather and Me

Today a hurricane threatens the eastern seaboard of the United States.

I used to think of weather as something outside of my life which every once in a while annoyed me by inserting itself into my space and making things ugly and uncomfortable, or pleased me by making things comfortable and beautiful.

More recently it struck me that weather and I share a symbiotic relationship in a larger context; weather doesn't invade my space, we share space.

Now, I am beginning to understand, that I am weather and weather is me.

Next, I will know, that there is no such thing as weather, and finally, I will understand, that there is no such thing as 'me.'

How to Teach Torah (in One Simple Lesson)

Humility is being 'you' and removing all of the stuff that isn't 'you.'

Once you do away with the layers of what you wish you were, or what you want others to think you are, or what others have insisted you are, and you just are, then you are humble.

If you run faster than anyone else in the world, it isn't arrogant to tell that to someone who just announced he needs someone who can run the fastest. If there is some disaster looming and a call goes out for the greatest genius to help resolve it, and you truly have the highest I.Q. in the world, it isn't haughty to make your I.Q. known.

Arrogance is bringing those things up when they don't matter. When they become 'who you are,' and not what you can do when the situation demands it.

I mention all of the above as an introduction to what I'm about to say:

Before a person can truly teach Torah, he must do away with his 'self;' his ego, that pesky voice that insists on living in a world of his own design, a world made up of what people think about him, and what he wants the world to think of him. When a humble person teaches Torah, there is only Torah. The goal of every teacher of Torah must be for their students to make direct and intimate contact with Torah. This is accomplished when the teacher receives Torah and then lives with humility.

The teacher then becomes a transparent vessel from which his students can drink.

Compared with the Torah itself, the greatest teacher is nothing; an ant when compared to the sun. Why introduce your students to an ant when they can have the sun?

Sadness

I used to hate Tisha B'Av. I hated its sadness and discomfort. I must be getting older because now I long for it to begin. A friend of mine died a few days ago. His death silently hangs in the air awaiting my attention.

Sadness is a part of the natural rhythm of life, but I rarely let it in. In the past it has always been an unwelcome guest in the domicile of my being because I associated it with depression. But now I see that sadness has been inappropriately found guilty by association, and I welcome it as a temporary lodger.

Tisha B'Av is about sadness and discomfort and death and the collapse of facades. These are important components of life without which there is only superficiality and emptiness.

We live in a most unusual time, a time when we believe we can choose not to endure pain or suffering. Many of us have come to believe that if people have pain, they made a mistake; they didn't take care of themselves, they should have rushed to the doctor, they hung around with the wrong people, etc. That is not necessarily true; death and separation and change are all a part of the rhythm of a well lived life. Basking in suffering, embracing sadness, and wallowing in self pity are unhealthy and should be discouraged. But allowing space for the pain of loss is something we must all learn to do if we are to fully actualize our time on this plane of existence.

And sometimes we really do need to learn lessons from our pain. Sometimes we do suffer because of mistakes we have made and we need to adjust our behavior to fix whatever is broken. Tisha B'Av is specifically focused on that kind of pain. We as a people suffered terribly on this day and many others. When we recall those events, we do so because we believe they could not have happened had we fully loved each other and G-d. Until we fix that, we remain in danger of adding to the list of events we mourn each year.

The citizens of the historical world would probably laugh and laugh if they read this; imagine people living at a time when they can even dream of not having to suffer.

The Revelation

I have a revelation to make. I make it because I trust you. I wouldn't tell this to just anybody. Most people would find this ridiculous and think me either mad or joking, but I sense that you are different. Your gaze is often fixed on deeper matters. You acknowledge the mundane but refuse to grant it more than its do. If I've misjudged you, I am sorry. The truth is, I must tell this to someone. I can't keep this to myself forever. The knowledge festers within me, and my only relief will come when I free it from its captivity within the narrow confines of my being. If I may, I would ask of you only one favor, that you read this to the end, before forming a fixed opinion. I promise it will not take up much of your time. I will be as brief and to the point as I am capable.

I am not of this world. I come from a place as far from here as is possible to imagine. I was formed of a substance that is so radically different from the material of this world; it is a wonder I can be here at all.

I am ancient. My longevity cannot be measured by any of the tools available. With my old age comes patience, hope, determination, and great wisdom gathered from the most profound sources of knowledge.

Please do not be confused by what I am about to say:

I am of this world. I do not just occupy a place in the Universe; I am made up of the very stuff of the Universe. I do not merely walk upon the earth; I am the earth. I am its mind, its conscience, and its articulate voice.

I am very young. With my youth comes naiveté, rebelliousness, a powerful lust for life, curiosity, and a clean slate ready to be written upon.

There are times when I experience conflict. I am faced with a circumstance that appears new and fresh. It suggests a myriad of mysterious possibilities; and yet, at the same time, I recognize it and remember encountering it many times before. It has laid itself bare to me. I know everything there is to know about it. Sometimes, when this happens, I remember that I see from two vantage points; and when I remember that, I am filled with a new awareness, one that helps me sort through the information before I engage the circumstance.

If I am both one thing and another, I must be two. Yet, somehow I manage my duality, which must make me three. But if I'm aware of my trebled nature, I must be four, and so on and so forth ad infinitum. I say all of this knowing with absolute certainty that I am really 'one', a very simple 'one', the simplest 'one' imaginable.

Thank you for your patience and your understanding. You have been kind to let me share my situation with you. It is here that it becomes uncomfortable, and somewhat awkward. I hope you don't think me forward, that I am somehow intruding into your affairs. As I've already said, you've been so kind to give me the time you already have. The truth is, I am intruding into your affairs; and if I am really sorry, I shouldn't be doing it. I guess this is it then, the awkward moment:

You see, I am you.

The Logic of Change

I remember sitting next to Gedalia, of blessed memory, in the dining room at Yeshivas Mishkan Hatorah. He studied classical languages at Harvard and was an expert not just in the languages, but also in classical literature and philosophy. One day, just to be funny, I asked him to explain the following:

How can it be that if you begin with two people who are exactly alike, which means that each one is exactly like the other; and just one of them changes, neither of them is alike. Somehow even though only one of them has changed, they've both changed? It defies logic.

He smiled softly, as was his way, but didn't say anything. The next day as we sat eating our lunches, he removed a slender volume from a plastic bag. It was a book on Logic written by Rabbi Moshe Chaim Luzatto. He opened it to a selected page and read a rule, which resolved my problem.

My sons are each beginning new chapters in their lives. The adventure is theirs and they go it, for the most part, alone. So why do I think, even though we are not exactly alike, that it's about me and my family and a new stage in our lives as well? Because it is, that's why.

Remembering

I have trouble remembering names. Not the names of people I have just met, but the names of people I already know, many of which I have known for a long time. I also find myself searching for a word that I know but can't access. I am assured by my friends and family that this is a normal part of aging. I believe them, sort of. There is a part of me that will always think that I'm the only one this is happening to, and it will remain afraid; afraid of what?

My grandparents all lost significant access to their memories before they died. Watching my parents deal with the loss of their parents' respective memories suggested a struggle with not only their parents' mortality, but their own. Something of my parents lived in the memories of their parents. They were carried like a soldier carries his wounded buddy from the battlefield, draped over his back, through mud and bush, over hills and through rivers. And when those memories were lost, my parents felt that a piece of their selves was lost as well.

One of the themes of Rosh Hashanah and Yom Kippur is that G-d remembers. Imagine that He didn't. On the one hand, I would feel relief. It would mean that He won't remember my failures, but then I would feel despair because He won't remember my triumphs either.

When G-d remembers those triumphs and failures they are real. Not just images from the past, but real, tangible, living material that I can still work with. I can change them, use them, plant them like seeds in the soil of my present, and nurture them as they grow into something more, new, and important. This is why Teshuva/repentance works. I'm not travelling back in some time machine to erase an event I wish never happened. I'm working on that very event now, in the present. I have it raised on a lift in the auto shop of my behavior, and I am fixing it in real time. All of that is only possible because G-d remembers. His memory of my triumphs and failures is a gift of me to me. It's up to me to make something of them.

Magic Moments

Several years ago my two older boys, A.Y. and Sruli, and I drove to Denver. Our stated purpose was to visit family, but it was clear to us that the real purpose was to have an adventure together. We had been travelling together every summer for several years and were getting better and better at it. Being good at travelling for us is not about precision planning and execution but about adapting to the rhythm of the trip and bonding with each other.

On the last day of the trip, just a few hours from home, the boys and I stood at the top of a tall, wooden, tower, just south east of Galena. The wind blew crisp with a touch of cool; and enjoying it even more than we was a family of hawks. They were gliding in and out of formation, often coasting by our tower perch. Down below two men sat on folding chairs, guiding remote controlled airplanes that mimicked the graceful gliding of the hawks and were, I imagined, a curious site to the hawks.

The moment was so wonderful; I couldn't help but comment to A.Y. and Sruli about how lucky we were that whenever we traveled we came upon such special moments. Before I finished, I realized it was no coincidence that we happened upon those moments. They were always there; we had just stopped to notice.

My Inner Child

There is a deep part of me, very, very, deeply hidden, like a child hidden for years in a dark cellar by his parents. This child has deep inner beauty, but is thought by his parents (some part of me plays the role of the parents) to be ugly; so they keep him out of sight and pretend he doesn't exist.

Every year at this time the sound of the shofar streaks like some jagged line of lightening, and strikes the heart of this boy, lighting up his cellar, and filling him with warmth and love. Several times, while driving on a long, flat, stretch of land, I have watched lightening strike. You can't tell; did the bolt of lightening originate in the clouds or from the ground? The shofar blast is like that. Does it originate in the shofar or in the heart?

Are You Kidding Me?

I imagine a child coming of age and really paying attention to the Rosh Hashanah liturgy for the first time. He is happily singing along, proud to participate in the various responsive readings, all the while reading and taking in the poetry and prose of the prayers. At one point he begins to look uncomfortable and unsure of himself. He looks around to see if others are equally perplexed, but finds them all blissfully engaged. He rereads the text just to make sure he had it right the first time, and then raises his hand for attention. The synagogue quiets down and looks towards the youth, who points to his prayer book and asks:

"Excuse me, this is the first time I've really had a good look at the text here, but am I right in understanding that there is a trial going on here, and that I could be sentenced to death?"

His fellow congregants nod, cough into their hands, and then assure him that Rosh Hashanah has always been about a trial, and that he would eventually get used to it. It is a little scary at first, but after a few years of nervously looking around every corner for his probable demise, he will, as they have, get used to the whole process and hardly worry at all.

"This trial," the boy would continue. "Where is it being held? Can I attend?"

Well no, of course he can't attend, he is told. It's held on high, in a realm not available to mortals.

"Will I be told what I'm accused of?"

Again, some nervous coughs and then a helpful congregant explains that the young man will have to take stock of himself and figure out what he might have done, and then assume that he stood accused of that action.

"When do I find out the verdict?" The boy asks.

Someone from a nearby seat explains that while he won't ever know for sure, he can assume that with the proper taking of stock and eventual repentance, he will be forgiven.

The boy will think for a moment and then say:

31

"I have never heard a tale more terrifying in my life. I am being told that I am to stand trial for crimes I can only guess at, in front of a secret tribunal that will have my life in their hands; and when it's ove,r I won't even know what they've decided! And all of you have known about this for years and yet you smile and sing and dip apples in honey. This is a nightmare! Why not do this around a campfire, at night, in the woods, and hold flashlights under your faces when you read from the siddur!"

The congregant closest to him puts his arm around the boy and assures him that it will be all right. He should just give it time; and before he knows it, Rosh Hashanah will become routine, and the fear will subside. And then the rest of the congregation goes back to their smiling and singing and apples dipped in honey.

Autumn in the Midwest

I love this time of year, the weather cools and the trees begin to reveal their true colors. With urgency we Midwesterners go about life, making the most of every moment, as winter looms on the horizon.

It is ironic how the leaves show so vibrant just as they prepare to die. We think of ourselves as leaves, and see their 'fall' as a metaphor for our last stage of life. But this is a mistake; because while our consciousness stubbornly insists on residing in the leaves of our lives, in truth we are actually trees. Fall is not our end, just a transition. Spring is not our beginning, but the continuation of a life reincarnated.

"Fortunate is the man ... who delights in the Torah of G-d, and in his Torah he meditates day and night. He will be like a tree planted by rivers of water that brings forth his fruit in season; his leaf shall not wither, and in whatever he does, he shall prosper" (Tehilim/Psalms 1).

"G-d blessed them and G-d said to them, 'Be fruitful and multiply, fill the earth and subdue it; and rule over the fish of the sea, the bird of the sky, and every living thing that moves on the earth.'" (Breishit/Genesis 1/28)

Our creativity is in part described as fruit, because we are trees. There are years, when we are first growing, when no fruit appears. During those years we tend and protect with the anticipation of fruit in the future. When we mature and begin to bear fruit, even then the first stage is bare branches, then buds, then unripe fruit, all with the anticipation of fruit; and finally the fruit is ripe, quickly harvested and brought to market. This fruit is eventually eaten, many of its seeds planted, only to grow more trees, bearing fruit ad infinitum.

Our holidays, Pesach, Shavuot, and Succot follow this progression. Pesach is the holiday of the spring, first buds. Shavuot is the holiday when the first fruits appear, and Succot the holiday when we celebrate a successful harvest. Each year we pay attention to this cycle because it not only describes the cycle of our livelihood, it also describes the cycle of our lives as creative beings.

From the Mouth of Hamlet

A few years ago my son, Moishe, and I went to see Hamlet. The theater was out of doors in a hilly, tree filled, part of Wisconsin. The weather was crisp, the trees were just beginning to wear their fall colors, the sky was blue, and the play was magnificent. We went because Moishe and I read Hamlet together; and I promised Moishe that when we had the chance, we would see the play.

One of the things I love about Shakespeare is how he puts the deepest thoughts into the mouths of the most unlikely characters. But there was a monologue from the mouth of Claudius, the evil king and uncle of Hamlet, that truly stunned us; especially as it was in the midst of the Rosh Hashanah, Yom Kippur, season:

"...My fault is past. But, O, what form of prayer

Can serve my turn? 'Forgive me my foul murder'?

That cannot be; since I am still possess'd

Of those effects for which I did the murder,

My crown, mine own ambition and my queen.

May one be pardon'd and retain the offence?

In the corrupted currents of this world

Offence's gilded hand may shove by justice,

And oft 'tis seen the wicked prize itself

Buys out the law: but 'tis not so above;

There is no shuffling, there the action lies

In his true nature; and we ourselves compell'd,

Even to the teeth and forehead of our faults,

To give in evidence. What then? what rests?

Try what repentance can: what can it not?

Yet what can it when one can not repent?

O wretched state! O bosom black as death!

O limed soul, that, struggling to be free,

Art more engaged! Help, angels! Make assay!

Bow, stubborn knees; and, heart with strings of steel,

Be soft as sinews of the newborn babe!

All may be well.

Rising] My words fly up, my thoughts remain below:

Words without thoughts never to heaven go. (Hamlet, Act III, Scene III)"

If only Jews hadn't been expelled from England during Shakespeare's age, he might have learned what we all rely on at this time of year; that you only have to take the first step towards change, and then G-d's help kicks in.

Succot in St. Louis

One Succot I visited the Arch, in St. Louis. Sruli, Moishe, Shauli, several nieces and nephews, and I occupied one of several tiny elevator modules, and eventually spilled onto the observation deck, point, place, thing.

It was a clear Fall day and the vistas were magnificent to behold. There was the grand Mississippi river below with barges pushing along its muddy waters, there were the tall reflecting structures of steel and glass of downtown, and the multi colored, tree covered, hills, to the west.

The children popped from one window to the next, shouting and pointing.

"Look how small the people look."

"There's a boat, see, there it is."

"Where's the bathroom?"

It reminded me of moments in the Sukkah, a spiritual vantage point with its own remarkable vistas, when during a holiday meal, a few of the adults would take in the scene: The crisp cool air, children chattering, the remnants of a delicious feast marking the spot where piles of sweet smelling food once laid. We would look at each other and someone would say:

"Look at this, is this not magnificent."

Aristotle and Me

I'll bet you, that in the past few months I've been exposed to more information than Aristotle was during his entire lifetime. Yet, I am no Aristotle. How can that be?

In fertile, well tilled, soil, one seed can become a majestic tree, bearing fruit that will in turn bear seed filled fruit, which will find their way into the soil, and themselves become majestic fruit bearing trees, ad infinitum. In unfertile, hard, soil (my mind), a million seeds can fall, without one of them taking root. Once a seed has taken root, it must be treated with patience and care. Majestic fruit bearing trees do not grow overnight

Rav Moshe Shapiro once taught us, that while other cultures use spring as a metaphor for childhood, the Talmud considers winter the appropriate metaphor. Spring is the time of the first budding of the flowers, the time when plants break through the surface of the earth; but before that happens, hidden beneath the surface, life begins to stir. So winter is actually the first stage of life, and spring is when you begin to see the flowering of that life.

That first stage of life is very delicate, that is why it takes place in a protected environment. It is nurtured with patience and great care.

Winter is designed for just this process. It is dark and cold. Life turns inward, and moves slowly. I struggle with winter. I don't want to look inward, to nurture, to slow down. I want to expand, to move outward, to race towards pleasure, and bask in its warm light. But when I struggle with winter, I am struggling with a powerful rhythm of life; and as always happens when I struggle with forces of that magnitude, I will loose. So why not just accept winter for what it is, and join its course; and maybe, just maybe, I'll nurture something significant, and make up some of the distance between Aristotle and me.

Letting Things Take Time

I used to wonder; what did Noach and his family do to pass the time in the Ark?

There is a Midrash which teaches that they spent their entire time in the Ark taking care of the animals. According to Rabbi Dessler z'l this was not just something to do; it satisfied an essential requirement for the re-emergence of mankind, 'chesed/loving kindness.' As King David remarked: "The world is built by Chesed (Tehilim/Psalms 89/3)." The new post-flood world would germinate in an environment of pure chesed.

But then it occurred to me that I was also bothered by why they needed to be in the Ark for such a long time; they didn't actually touch ground for a year after the rains began? And for that matter, why did it take so long to build that Ark?

Later I realized that what was really bothering me was an issue I have been struggling with for many years, and that was: letting things take time. Transitions take time. You need to build a "vessel" that will contain the 'change.' That's why a fetus has to spend so much time developing in the womb. That's why a child takes so long to become a viable contributing member of society. That's why people had to live so long at the dawn of life on earth. That's why the Jewish People had to spend so much time in the desert before entering the Land of Israel. And finally, that's why I have to wait six weeks to get the first issue of my Sporting News subscription.

Soaring

We were singing Passover songs around the table. I closed my eyes and an image of me, my arms wrapped in heavy link chain attached to the ground, appeared before me. I was certain that no matter how hard I would struggle with those chains, I would not have been able to wrest myself free of them. Truth be told, I wasn't struggling. Somehow I understood that my chains were forged from my 'fear of soaring.' This was the spiritual equivalent of the 'fear of flying.'

But then the song began to envelop me and at one point beckoned to my adventurous aspect, which then took charge for a brief moment and opened up what was only a crack in my armor of self control. The song seeped through the crack, cool and soothing, and found its way to a very deep place. Without warning, my chest burst open and out soared a snow-white dove. It took off, straight up and then turned backward on itself describing a glorious loop afterward gliding effortlessly in a giant counterclockwise sweep of a white sky. It struck me that I was that dove, but for some reason I was watching it soar and glide from my perch on the ground.

Somehow, with just that realization, that I was the dove, I was soaring together with the dove. We rose at great speed, facing each other, racing to some 'no place.' It then struck me that if the dove were me I shouldn't be looking at it, I should be seeing through its eyes. With that thought I was seeing the world through the dove's eyes. For a brief moment my eyes were the dove's eyes. It was then that whatever part of my being was supposed to be in charge of my 'fear of soaring' regained control of the ship, and shut everything down. I tried to continue seeing through the dove's eyes, but I couldn't get it back. I couldn't even see the dove.

You would think that I would be sad, with the image gone and myself once again firmly chained to the earth. But I was not because having gone there once, I knew the secret of how to get there again.

(The secret is lulling that part of me that controlled my 'fear of soaring' to sleep, and once I've done that ...I'm off.)

Friday Night Mayhem

Once, when my family lived in Maalot Dafna (a suburb of Jerusalem), my sons and I found ourselves in the middle of the frightening chaos of a Shabbat demonstration.

It was a Friday night and three of my sons (ages 6-10) and I accompanied students from Ohr Somayach on a tour of some local chassidic tisches (literally "table," a tisch is a wonderful event common amongst most chassidim, held on Friday nights. The Rebbe eats his meal together with his chassidim, who have returned after eating their own private family meals. There's beautiful singing and powerful words from the Rebbe. When attending one I always felt transported to a place I experienced as the soul of Shabbos).

On our way to the Tisches, we saw a large group of people gathered to prevent driving on Shmuel HaNavie Street, not far from the infamous Bar Ilan Street. I approached a policeman and informed him that in a nearby building there were over a thousand chassidim celebrating a tische with a visiting Rebbe, that he shouldn't provoke them or there would be a catastrophe. Maybe just that night they could close the street. He told me that he couldn't do that. It was his job to protect people's rights to drive on a public thoroughfare. I pleaded with him, but he wouldn't listen. Just then a young woman driving a small car, maybe a mini, drove by. A crowd of several hundred people surrounded her car, forcing it to stop, and started shaking it back and forth. Several large students from Ohr Somayach and I approached the group and shouted at them to stop, helping the girl out of the car. The look in their eyes, rage with no empathy, was frightening. The girl was in shock and went to the protection of the police officers, who looked at me with a look that said, what kind of animals are you people?

We then left for the tisches. A few hours later we returned. When we arrived at the park in front of Ohr Somayach, there was pandemonium. Riot police on horses were riding through with truncheons beating fleeing chassidim. I was terrified that my sons and I would be hurt. We literally feared for our lives. We found a large boulder and hid behind it until the coast was clear; then we ran home as fast as we could.

My children and I talk about that moment often. I hope we never see something like that again.

Single Minded

I heard a man tell of his life after a brain injury. Eventually he was healed, but there was a time when he could focus on only one thing at a time. This caused him a great deal of emotional distress. But he said that there was one benefit. When he ate or smelled or saw something special, the experience was intensely pleasurable. It became the focus of his entire being. Imagine what it would be like if we could focus on only one thing, and it was G-d.

Blissful Anonymity

Several years ago I walked in Chicago's downtown from a parking garage to the Israeli Consulate to renew my passport. I planned to walk along Michigan Avenue, past the Wrigley building, over the river, and then on to Wacker Drive. On a whim I took the stairs to a lower level, and walked underneath Michigan Avenue instead. What I entered was another world.

I left a colorful, bustling, vibrant, thoroughfare for a dank, grey, world of service entrances and homeless people sleeping on cardboard. I felt suddenly nameless and faceless. No one knew who I was, nor would they care who I was in that place. All matters of station and bearing were blanketed by the thick, bleak, shadows of that underworld. If the 'downtown' was the heart of Chicago, I was in its intestines, and it stank... at first; but then I began to like it. I liked not having to project self importance, not caring what others thought of me. I liked the democracy of a place where all were equally insignificant. I felt genuine relief and relaxation, like some heavy burden had been lifted.

That, of course, lasted for just a moment. I eventually ascended on the other side of Wacker Drive and walked into the gleaming sky scraper that housed the Israeli Consulate, and presented myself to the information desk. There I was asked to produce identification so that I could be admitted to the consulate, where they would process documents that would satisfy the curiosity of even the most demanding of inquisitors, explaining to everyone, who I was, in the most official way.

Listening

When I listen, I mean really listen, I become a vessel and pay attention as the information flows from the speaker and enters me. I am a receiver. I don't judge the information, I don't extrapolate from it, I don't question it; I just receive it. My goal, while I'm listening, is to make space for whatever the other person or entity wishes to pour into me and to contain every last drop of it, nothing more.

This is the process for receiving the Torah. I open up space for it. I don't judge it. I don't criticize it. I don't try to make it into something in my image. Once I have received it, it will inform me, it will mold me, it will be what it is, and no amount of my meddling and fixing and decorating will ever make it into more than that.

Ordinary Power

My friend Willy visited for a few days. We have been friends for years. We were chavrutot/study partners, and remain dear friends. We reminisced about many fond times together. I went to London for his wedding; each day of that trip was an adventure. He traveled around the U.S. via Greyhound, and spent four days in Milwaukee and Chicago, during which time, I was his tour guide. We got drunk once on a bottle of Arak, and I still feel nauseated when I get near the stuff. We climbed down Nachal Darja, an intricate chain of rope descents and mountain hiking, in a dry riverbed, near Ein Gedi. We laughed and cried together. He spent time with my family and got to know them, and I spent time with his, and get to know them. After we married we would visit each other, our wives became friends. We shared many common, (and some not so common), friends.

But, what struck me the other day, while the two of us were running through old times, was that the deepest and most meaningful thing we ever did together, was learn. We learned the commentary of the Ramban on Chumash/Torah. We learned for over two years, and I often refer back to lessons learned during those sessions. It didn't seem dramatic at the time, but that seems to be the way of the deepest things. At first they seem ordinary and simple, only to eventually reveal their immense stature.

This is not a Zero Sum Game

Many a person looks at their relationship with G-d as a zero sum game. In their worldview you begin with a clean slate and then anything you do wrong puts you in disfavor with G-d. If you are imperfect, He is unhappy with you.

This might be a good attitude to help you strive for perfection, which is an admirable goal and requires extreme measures and attitudes, as long as you don't really believe that with G-d you're either perfect or a disappointment.

A good mentor will be tough with you while he motivates you to excellence. He may say things that he knows will push you to fight harder against adversity, or to pull yourself up after you've fallen, but they are never meant as an objective assessment of your value. They are not a real indication of his true feelings for you.

It is a common mistake to confuse one for the other, but it's a mistake all the same.

When Leader's Rebuke

Fourteen years ago, a small political party in Israel, Degel Hatorah, threatened to pull out of an extremely fragile coalition. The party had two Knesset members, and the government had only a one-seat majority. If the small party pulled out of the coalition, the government would collapse. The party's spiritual Mentor was Rabbi Eliezer Man Shach. Rav Shach was, while himself the Rosh Hayeshiva (Dean) of a prestigious yeshiva, the defacto head of the Yeshiva movement. Israelis in general knew him as the embodiment of the "Charedi" movement.

During the same time that the Degel Hatorah party was considering pulling out of the coalition, they were to hold their annual convention. At any other time this convention would draw scant attention. Maybe it would have been attended by a few hundred people. That year they had to rent out a stadium, Yad Eliyahu. Fifteen thousand people attended in person, and the rest of the country watched on television or listened on the radio.

The most famous radio and TV personalities covered the event. There was deep background, color commentary, and man on the street interviews. Everyone was going to watch or listen to Rav Shach's speech, hoping to glean information about the future of the government. He would speak for about a half an hour, and just about every Jew in Israel would be paying attention.

I remember wondering what he would say. Not about the coalition, but what would he say to the Jews of Israel. After all, he was a Jewish leader and had been for decades. He was 95 years old, at the end of his life. What would he say to the Jews of Israel? He had never had an opportunity to speak to everyone before and would never have another one, what would he say?

What he said, surprised, shocked and in the beginning, disappointed me. He rebuked the nation. His tone was loving but his theme was essentially; "How have we gotten to this place? A place where a child could grow up in the Land of Israel and never see a synagogue, and more of the like." I kept on saying to myself he should have been supportive, motivational, and gentle with the people. He was none of those.

After the event the talk shows were on fire with the livid response to his rebuke. Who was he to tell people what to do ....?

A few weeks later I mentioned my thoughts to a friend of mine, how I was disappointed that Rav Shach chose to use his opportunity to speak to every Israeli, to rebuke them. He told me he saw it differently; after all, Rav Shach's words had informed the national discussion for several weeks. Everyone was talking about the national character from one perspective or another. He shook us up. True, there were many people angry with what he said; but maybe his goal wasn't that people be happy, but that they wake up and do something.

It recently dawned on me that Moshe does the same thing. The book of Devarim (Deuteronomy) is Moshe's parting monologue before the people, and it is for the most part rebuke. There he was at the end of his life and his last words are stinging rebuke. He too must have felt that even at the dusk of his life, it was his role to wake us up and not care about who got angry. He was then, as he always had been, our leader, and it was his job to move us forward.

The Art of War

"All warfare is based on deception. Hence when able to attack, we must seem unable; when using our forces, we must seem inactive; when we are near, we must make the enemy believe we are far away; when far away, we must make him believe we are near. Hold out bait to entice the enemy. Feign disorder, and crush him. If he is secure at all points, be prepared for him. If he is in superior strength, evade him," Yosef read from a bent notebook he kept in his shirt pocket. "It's all here; simple, elegant, and so obviously true."

"What are you talking about?" I asked, leaning forward over the table for two, at the pizza shop that was our regular venue for philosophical debate.

"I'm talking about a strategy to overcome, you know, the enemy."

"The enemy."

"Yeah, the enemy. You know, The Enemy, with a capitol E."

"No Yosef, I don't know, 'The Enemy' with a capitol E."

"Oh I get it, you're practicing what I was just reading, making him think we don't know about him, the deception. I'm with you."

"No, I'm not practicing deception, I really don't know what you're talking about," I said as I returned to sitting back in my chair.

"Oh, right; what an idiot. If I say that you're practicing deception then he'll figure the whole thing out. O.K., I got it, you don't know what I'm saying," Yosef says with a dramatic wink.

"Forget it. Where did you find that quote?" I asked, trying to steer the discussion in a more fruitful direction.

"Sun Tzu's, 'The Art of War'. It was written in China two thousand five hundred years ago. It's a manual for generals or just people who need a strategy to overcome an opponent. I saw a copy of it and immediately recognized that this was just what I needed to overcome... 'You know who'." When he said, "you know who", he learned forward and whispered.

I leaned forward until my face was about six inches from his face, and whispered back;

"Why are we whispering?"

"Oh, yeah, deception; I keep on forgetting. Don't worry; I'll get the hang of this. You know; you picked this up pretty quickly. Have you read the "Art of War" before?" Yosef asked as he looked at his grease-covered menu.

I don't know why he always looked at the menu. We had been meeting at the pizza shop every week for twenty-five years, ever since our freshman year in high school, when we first became chavrutot.

"No, I never read the "Art of War', but it does sound interesting. What else does he write?" I asked. The waiter came just then, and I ordered vegetarian chili covered with cheese. Yosef spent a full minute going over the menu and ordered what he ordered every week for the twenty-five years we had been meeting;

"I think I'll have a slice of pizza and an order of cheddar fries. And ... a diet coke, no ice." Then he put the menu down and flipped to the next page in his notebook.

"Here's another good one: 'Therefore the skillful leader subdues the enemy's troops without any fighting; he captures their cities without laying siege to them, he overthrows their kingdom without lengthy operations in the field. With his forces intact he will dispute the mastery of the Empire, and thus, without losing a man, his triumph will be complete.'

"Are you talking about the Yetzer Hara? Is he 'The Enemy'?" I asked finally getting it.

"There goes the whole deception thing. Why don't you just scream it out loud so everybody will know."

"I wasn't practicing deception; I didn't know what you were talking about. So you're saying that you want to apply 'The Art of War' to battling the Yetzer Hara. I like that. That's actually quite clever. Not bad, Yosef, not bad," I said genuinely impressed. "What's your plan, how are you going to implement it?"

Yosef picked up his menu so that it blocked his face entirely. "The first thing I'm going to do is to stop sharing my plans with you."

Simple Power

Rabbi Bentzion Brook was the Rosh Hayeshiva/Dean of the Nevardok Yeshiva, in Jerusalem. He would speak to us once a week when I studied at Yeshivat Mishkan Hatorah. At that time he was already in his nineties. He was short and thin, with a small white beard and a well lined, pale face. He walked with a limp, the result of a bomb exploding during one of Israel's early wars. We would all be sitting at our study tables when he walked in. We would stand for him and wait for him to sit at a table facing us. He walked very slowly and deliberately, his arm supported by my teacher and mashgiach/spiritual mentor, Rabbi Asher Rubinstein. Rav Asher had studied with Rav Bentzion for several years, and it was due to their relationship that Rav Bentzion came to speak with us. He was speaking to the students of his student.

Once he took his seat he would look us over with a beautiful smile, and then slowly open a large tome of Gemara/Talmud that was waiting for him on the desk. His lectures were almost always a reading of the Gemara. Generally, he would add very little of his own. He knew that he didn't have to; the Gemara was powerful enough. Sometimes he would tell us what it was like to be a student in the great pre-war Nevardok yeshivos, or explain a point of Mussar/ethical instruction, but for the most part his presentation was very simple. His life, for that matter, was very simple.

He lived in a sparse apartment in the Nevardok yeshiva building. He had very few possessions. One Purim some friends and I visited him; and one of us, Gershon, offered him some champagne. He drank it and laughed when the bubbles tickled his nose. He told us he never had champagne before. I once visited him in the hospital after he had injured his already injured leg and brought flowers to decorate his room for Shabbos. He was genuinely puzzled by the flowers; they seemed such an extravagance to him.

His simplicity allowed the power of his Torah to be all the more apparent. When he read, even just literally read, a selection from the Gemara to us, I was often blown away, sometimes frightened, most times exuberant.

He showed me, that when I teach, the most valuable thing I can do for my students is get out of the way and allow them to make simple contact with Torah.

Keeping Kosher in the New Millenium

I am often asked about the seemingly obsessive-compulsive nature of people who keep Kosher. Why the people of today can't be like the people of forty and fifty years ago, when Kashrut observance seemed so much more natural and simple?

When I look at my own observance, I recognize the legitimacy of the rebuke to a certain degree; there is certainly room for reflection on my attitude to Kashrut observance. But lately I find the question interesting because it suggests that many of us are in denial about the nature of what we eat. It demonstrates how we have come to accept what has become an extremely complicated, multi-tiered system of food preparation and delivery. This relies on so many people in so many places doing so many things, which we think of as normal and simple. The truth is that the manner in which most of the food we eat is prepared and produced is so complicated one needs scientific training just to understand it. What is in your food and how it got to you is no longer intuitive. You are shocked when you find out what is in your food and shocked to know the details of how it was produced.

We rarely experience this shock because, for most of us, our food grows on supermarket shelves. Salad is no longer made up of vegetables that grow in our gardens or farms, it is made up of sliced produce that is wrapped and often mixed in bags after having come in contact with chemical fertilizers and pesticides and mysterious processes to increase their shelf lives. They may never have touched the earth; and if they did, it could have been earth from anywhere on the planet.

It could be argued that it is not Kashrut which is essentially complicated; it is the manner in which we prepare our food that is. Kashrut is just trying to keep up with how we eat and it's then that the issues of trust and concern for the minutia arise. If I am five steps removed from the source of my food, I need to know who the other four steps are, or I need to rely on someone else to do that for me. If I look at the ingredients on the side of an Entenmans box, I need a degree in food chemistry just to know what they are, or I need to rely on someone else who does. And then I need people to assure me that what they say is in there, is all that is in there, or is really what is in there.

Therefore, one answer to why the people of today can't be like the people of forty and fifty years ago, when Kashrus observance seemed so much more natural and simple, is because eating is no longer simple.

Heavenly Detention

I had the following day-dream:

I am sitting on a small, kindergarten sized chair, alone, in a gigantic room. On the door is an appropriately gigantic sign, which reads, "Detention." I have a vague sense that I'm being punished, but I'm not sure why. Suddenly the door opens, and another guy sheepishly enters, and sits himself down on an equally undersized chair. At first we don't make eye contact, we just awkwardly stare forward at the bare walls of the detention room. After a few moments, I turn to him; and not wanting to betray my ignorance as to what is happening, I ask him what he's in for. He turns to me and says:

"I was being tested. You know, a "life test." I own a stationary business, wholesale, and I had an opportunity to buy a large quantity of stock at an incredibly low price. There was no way the stuff was legit, it had to be stolen merchandise. So I thought about it for a few days and ..."

"You bought the merchandise, and now you're being punished." I finish in anticipation of the end of his story. I have the annoying habit of finishing other people's thoughts for them.

"No, not at all, I didn't buy the stuff; I knew it was the wrong thing to do."

"So then why are you in detention?" I ask.

"Because I cheated on the test; my older brother had the same thing happen to him last year, and he gave me the answer from his test," he answers, embarrassed.

"How did you get caught?" I ask.

"I had crib notes, and they fell out of my pocket just as I refused the sale."

"Ah, a classic case of fallen crib notes. That'll get you detention every time." I say, empathetically.

"Yeah, I knew it was risky, but I was afraid that when it came time to say no, I would blank, or freeze, or something. Next time I'm writing it on my hand in ink. It's a lot safer."

"I agree."

Who are we?

It struck me a day or two ago, that when we are identified to be called up to the Torah or a Mishabeirach is said for us, we are described as so and so the son or daughter of so and so. We are identified by who our parents are, not by what we do for a living, where we are from, what we look like, or how old we are; just by who our parents are.

The Comfortable Life

It struck me, not too long ago, that I value comfort not just as a context, but as an ethic. If I plan an event and disregard the comfort of others, I have done something wrong, not just foolish. Comfort has entered the realm of right and wrong, good and bad.

Not every culture values comfort the way our culture does: European beer has a bite to it that is uncomfortable to the American palette, so popular American beers remove the offending taste. We end up with a less full-bodied flavor, but no bite. Mediterranean olives have a bitter taste that Americans have removed; we are left without the bitterness, but we lose the layers of flavor that the Mediterranean olive contains. Our hotels and motels are clean and comfortable, but in the process of achieving reliable, uniform, comfort, we have left out the "heimishness" that could be found in the bed and breakfast or inns. We have proven over and over, that we are willing to sacrifice layers of experience for the sake of comfort.

This practice of sacrificing depth of experience to avoid discomfort has found its way into my spiritual life as well. There have been many moments that could have been deep and meaningful, but because they would have been uncomfortable I avoided them. For example, I want my Shabbos to have a certain quality, I want my family time to have a certain quality, and to have that disturbed by people or places that would not contribute to the desired atmosphere would be too uncomfortable, spiritually uncomfortable, so I avoid them. When I give in to my desire for comfort, what I end up with is the 'American beer' of family time, the 'Holiday Inn' of Shabboses; comfortable but sterile.

Pushing the Envelope

Sometimes you need to push the envelope, but how do you know when to push and when to surrender? If you push and you're denied, it hurts. It is painful to be told no.

Moshe (Moses) was an envelope pusher. It was a unique quality of his relationship with G-d. You just don't find people who were told by G-d to stop, that they were getting too close. Moshe was told that at the Burning Bush. Later on he asked G-d to see His face, and G-d had to tell him that he couldn't, but he could see him from behind, etc. And then at the end of his life he asked G-d to let him into the land and G-d said no, but that He would give him a tour from afar.

There are two types of envelope pushers: The first has a thick skin and little empathy, he is unfazed by a 'no' because he doesn't really care what the other person thinks. The second type has great empathy and a very thin membrane but is humble. His humility allows him to hear the 'no', to accept it for what it is, and not interpret it as a judgement about his value. Moshe was the humblest of all men, so he could handle rejection.

Maybe that's the answer. You don't have to know for sure that you'll get what you want when you push, you just need to be humble for the times you're told 'no'.

The Zone

Sometimes you experience a magical moment; you're "in the zone." After experiencing those moments several times, you begin to realize that you aren't really at that place; you're just getting a glimpse of it, so that you know what to strive for.

Rabbi Twerski once taught a Chassidishe reading, of a Midrash, quoted by Rashi, on the first Possuk/Verse in Parshas

Vayeitze (Genesis 28/10). The Midrash explains that when a Tzadik leaves a place, it leaves a void. The Hebrew words for 'leaves a void' are "Oseh Roshem;" which can also be translated as "makes a mark."

The first Posuk in Vayeitze is describing Yaakov's departure from Israel, to his uncle's home in Charan. He anticipated difficulty and a significant drop in spirituality. What does a Tzadik do when he finds himself in a place that he wants to be, but he knows he can't remain there? He marks the way (like Hansel and Gretel marked the path home with bread crumbs), so that he will eventually be able to find his way back.

Look Over There

There are teachings that point out an idea and are not meant to be an end in themselves.

Have you ever tried pointing a dog in a particular direction, only to be frustrated, because the dog won't take its attention off of your finger? You stubbornly shout: "No, no, that way, look that way!" But the dog remains glued to your finger.

Midrash is like that. The particular teaching points at an idea. You miss the point if you refuse to take your eyes off of the words (insist on a literal interpretation), instead of looking in the direction the teaching is pointing.

Standing in Line

I stood on line in the Greyhound bus terminal, in St. Louis. There were several lines forming. One line of people waited for a bus to Los Angeles and several cities along the way, another to New York and several cities along the way. There was a line of people waiting for a bus to Miami and all points in between, and so on. Because the lines formed just a few feet from each other, there was lots of casual, cross-line conversation, until an announcement would come over the speaker system, and a line of people disappeared. As I watched a line disappear, I thought of how they would end up in some dramatically different place from me, even though we stood side by side, just feet from each other, in the bus terminal.

Several years ago, I stood on line at the Central Bus Station in Jerusalem, waiting for a bus home. Israel was just beginning to introduce buses with air conditioning, some had it installed and some didn't. I imagined deciding to take the next air conditioned bus, even if it was to Eilat, just because it was air conditioned. When I arrived in Eilat, I would call Tzippy (my wife), and she would ask me where I was. I would tell her Eilat, and when she asked me if I was crazy, I would say: I boarded the bus because it had air conditioning.

How many times have I chosen a path because it was comfortable, with no care about where it lead?

Lessons Learned at the Liquor Store

When I was little, five or six, my great-grandfather, Abe Gecht, owned several liquor stores. I would often visit my great-grandparents, who lived in an apartment on top of one of the stores, White Manor Liquors. I remember my great-grandfather coming upstairs with the money earned that day and counting it at the kitchen table; he would let me count the 'ones.' My great-grandmother, Ida, would bake strudel, and challah rolls, and cookies, and the seductive smell would waft from the oven. When she had just taken them out, and they were still warm, she would call me over for a taste. They were soft and sweet and filled with love. I loved visiting them and still cherish the memories.

One of my favorite activities at the liquor store was to help the workers put away the empty beer bottles. There was a conveyer belt next to the cash registers. When someone would return a case of empty beer bottles, the box would be sent down to a lower floor via the conveyer belt, on to a platform with rollers, where it would wait to be stored. Below the retail part of the store was a huge warehouse filled with new stock waiting to be shelved and space to store the hundreds of cases of empties. I knew where each brand belonged and took pride in putting them in their respective stacks. There were Blatz, and Hamms, and Old Milwaukee, and Schlitz, and Gettleman, and many more.

On the sales floor, there were rows and rows of liquor. The store was set up like a supermarket, every shelve stocked with liquor. At the back of the store there were stacks of full cases of beer. The cases were stacked five or six high and maybe twenty wide. When people wanted to buy a case of beer, they went to the back wall and picked up a case and placed it in their shopping cart. I'm not sure when I first discovered this, but at some point I found that I could climb the beer cases and then find empty spaces that formed tunnels. I would climb through those tunnels out of the view of my great-grandfather, my uncle and my grandfather, who worked there as well, and I would be occupied for hours. Sometimes I would be tunneling, and I would look out through the holes made to lift the beer cases, through the bottles, and out the holes on the other side; and I could watch the customers as they shopped. There were a couple of times that I thought they were going to take the very case of beer I was looking through, and then I would be caught. I don't know what I thought would happen if I were caught; they would have probably fainted from the shock of suddenly seeing a little boy appear from behind a case of beer.

Those skills learned at my great-grandparents have served me well. They taught me to take disparate ideas and put them in their place, and then once they are all stacked up, to travel the myriad of tunnels that run through them; and most important, to take time to taste the malt.

My Embarrassment

The other day I was embarrassed. I did something or actually didn't do something I was supposed to, and I was embarrassed. People were angry and I had to spend several hours with them while their anger was good and hot. I don't like being embarrassed and I didn't like it then. The question was how to escape the embarrassment. I didn't have to wait long; within a few short minutes I found an excuse to be angry;

ahhhh… relief, no more embarrassment, just good old anger. But the pleasure of anger didn't last long, I'm such a fool when I'm angry and I was a fool then; and before I knew it, I was back to being embarrassed, but then I had more to be embarrassed about. It was then that I caught myself. I didn't have to escape it. It was not attacking me. I would not die from shame. So I just let it be. I experienced it as something interesting, like a dramatic cloud formation or a gnarled twisted willow. The embarrassment wasn't me, it was a feeling that simply arose in me, and after drifting for a while in my vicinity, like an early morning fog after the sun came up, it was gone.

What is a Prophet?

A Navie (prophet) is not unlike an audio or visual tuner. As I sit in front of my computer, alone in my office, I am aware that there are countless waves of energy moving along electromagnetic fields, filling the room with an endless potential of sounds and images. If I have the right tuner I can hear those sounds or see those images. The Navie (prophet) is just such a tuner for a spiritual equivalent to those electromagnetic waves.

Even if I am not yet a Navie and can't tune into the waves of energy traveling through the spiritual energy field, I can tune into your joy or sadness. I can hear your criticism or praise; I can see the glow of the aura of your being, as it chases away the darkness of your suffering.

A Story about Shabbos

Rabbi Michel Twerski of Milwaukee once told of a young man who visited his shul for the very first time. It was a Friday night, and a glance at the young man was all he needed to see that it was the first time the young man had ever been in an Orthodox shul, let alone one with a Chassidic Rabbi. The young man stared in wonder at the people and the service; and when it was time to leave, Rabbi Twerski asked him if he would like to come home with him for a Shabbat dinner. The visitor quickly accepted the Rabbi's invitation. It was then that the Rabbi asked him if he would mind emptying his pockets.

When telling the story, Rabbi Twerski explained that he didn't know why he asked him to empty his pockets. It was not his style to push things on people he didn't think they were ready for, but it just came out. Understandably, the young man was puzzled by the request; but after being assured that his belongings would be safe, he put them away and then joined the Rabbi for the walk to his home. Shortly after they began to walk, the visitor asked Rabbi Twerski why he had been asked to empty his pockets.

The Rabbi paused to frame his response. Clearly the young man was not ready for an outline of the thirty-nine categories of forbidden labor on Shabbat, one that did not allow carrying objects in a public domain or to and from a private domain. If he was going to answer him properly, it had to be an answer that would be meaningful to the young man then, at that moment. So the Rabbi asked him what he had in his pocket.

The young man said that he had his wallet, his car keys, and some loose change. The Rabbi then said, that on Shabbat G-d wanted to spend time with him, not with what kind of car he owned, or where his house was located, or how much money he had, which are all sometimes confused with who we are.

The Kotzker Rebbe once taught that Shabbat is related to a family of words which share the meaning: "to return." During the week we focus on doing, on Shabbat we return to simply being.

A Shortened Shiva

Several years ago, my grandfather, Shoyle, passed away. He died only a few days before Shavuot, and the shiva was shortened because of the holiday. My father was sitting shiva in Denver, and Rabbi Twerski flew in to be with him. He was staying at the home of his nephew, who at the time was the Rabbi of a nearby shul; and after he visited with my father, I walked him to his nephew's home. Rabbi Twerski had a migraine headache, and as irony would have it, there were men working at his nephew's home, noisily cutting marble tiles. But even in excruciating pain, he found the time to answer a question that had been bothering me.

Shiva makes so much sense. It gives us permission to take the time we need to come to terms with the loss of a loved one. Why would we cut it short because of a holiday?

He offered the following as a possible answer: While Shiva is a very profound tool for dealing with loss; it involves withdrawing from the everyday matters of life, which is something one should only do if there is no other choice. We are meant to be involved in life fully, with all of our being, and there is the danger of withdrawal that we will learn to opt out and stop contributing.

Shiva primarily deals with three issues facing the survivor. 1. Anger at G-d over the loss of the loved one. 2. Denial of the fact that the person is no longer there. 3. Guilt about enjoying life without the loved one. If you succeed at celebrating a Yom Tov/Holiday fully, two of those issues have been dealt with.

Anger can only be maintained within a narrow view of reality. When the cosmic picture of G-d's involvement with us and his loving kindness in such dramatic moments is brought to our attention, the anger dissipates.

Guilt is removed because you have not chosen to celebrate on your own; G-d commands you to celebrate. Once you've been able to do it, guilt free, you have a pattern to follow for future celebrations of life.

The only one that is not taken care of then, is denial. Perhaps, Rabbi Twerski suggested, the sages weren't willing to send us back into the withdrawal from life that is shiva, just for one reason, as important as that reason might be. And with that he looked, with resignation, towards the man cutting a particularly noisy piece of marble, and walked through the door of his nephew's home.

Learning from Prophets

In the past, when I have studied the works of the Prophets, I looked at them primarily from an academic perspective. I would study their words and the commentaries and compare them with the words of others, perhaps resolve conflicts with Jewish theology and history if there were any. My goal was a homogenous system of theology and history, from which I could draw my own theology and sense of Jewish history. They are, at their very least, the "Great Books" of Judaism, a canon which informs Jews and is the context in which we can have discussion and debate.

One example of a point of theology which I have drawn from the Prophets is that life in "this world," was meant to be "good," only "good" was meant to happen to us. If anything "bad" or "evil" occurred, it is out of the ordinary, a deviation from the status quo and had to be explained. According to the Prophets, the cause of that evil was our actions. Without getting into the issue of "why bad things happen to good people," this suggests that it does not require any extraordinary intervention for good to happen. Good is natural, it is the nature of the system itself; evil or bad are extraordinary and thus aberrations.

I began by saying "in the past," about studying the prophets from an academic perspective, because now I experience them differently when I read them. When I studied them in the past, the Prophets were an ancient, distant, work, and only with the help of commentaries was it even possible to approach them. It was as if the commentaries were some sophisticated listening device, reaching back thousands of years of history, and allowing me to eavesdrop on events and conversations that were happening to others. The problem was an experiential one; I felt a great distance between me and the Prophet, between me and the Prophet's teaching. Now, I enter the teaching without any intermediaries; he is talking to me. The commentaries are essential to understanding what is going on, but now I use them as an aide, rather than a go between.

Literacy

One of the reasons, arguably the least of reasons, to pursue Biblical literacy is for Jewish people to have a common corpus of literature to refer to when discussing issues of theology and morality. Now what we have, when discussing theology with most American Jews, is the highly problematic challenge of beginning with Christian theology and then distinguishing Judaism from that.

For instance: Hell. When speaking with an American Jew about Hell, you start something like this: "What image comes to mind when you think of Hell?" It will be something drawn from everything from "Dante's Inferno" to the Adam Sandler starrer, "Little Nicky." "O.K., we don't believe in a place like that, or a Devil like that." And then you must draw an equally compelling picture, of a much more subtle idea, a spiritual experience so distant from our physical world that it can only be described in poetry, in order to replace the default image that the person began with.

This is why I think that when we set a goal for Jewish literacy in our schools, we should not be satisfied with a vague familiarity with Biblical text; rather, that the Torah should be the context from which the student looks out at the rest of the world.

Dumb Children

My friend, Bob, shared something his father said from time to time, usually after returning from dinner with family friends. He would sit at the table or in a chair, look over his family, and pronounce: "I must be the only father in this city with dumb children."

They would all laugh. They laughed because they knew what he meant, that so many parents have become not only activity directors for their children, but publicity agents. These parents believe that a proper image must be cultivated for their children, so that they can get into the 'right' schools, and introduced into the 'proper' society, all so that the parents themselves can be seen as 'successful.' It is in their role as publicist for their children that these parents cite every achievement, public service, grade point average, test score, elected office, and athletic performance. For the children this means that they must live like members of a Royal family, with a contrived public image, and a secret personal life. And G-d protect you if you cannot live up to the necessary public image. It also means that when communicating priorities to our children, parents pass over principles of basic goodness in favor of demonstrable indications of success.

It is in light of the above that I take comfort in the Ten Commandments. They represent the only communication directly made by G-d to the entire Jewish people. There are so many things He could have said. He could have talked about lofty, sublime ideas, he could have waxed poetic, kabalistic, or philosophical. He could have outlined levels of achievement that would indicate success and accomplishment in the spiritual realm.

Have you ever attended a lecture given by an academic or theologian? Unless you yourself have had academic training, their ideas are enigmatic, mysterious, opaque, and downright unintelligible. But not G-d, his message is simple and straightforward.

Abraham Lincoln's Gettysburg Address was 266 words long (according to some it was 272 words long). It took him three minutes to deliver it. The Ten Commandments are 172 words (in Hebrew) long, and if spoken by Lincoln, would have taken two minutes to communicate. They are about the simple things that matter most, the things that get lost in our drive towards sophistication and theological accomplishment. They are about the things that eventually knock the 'Kings' off of the 'hills' of success.

It's almost as if G-d is saying that other stuff matters, but never take your eyes off of these. Wouldn't it be nice if we could do the same for our children, if we could point to the Torah and say, this is what matters, don't sweat the other stuff?

An Unlikely Martyr

While studying the various issues raised by Korach's rebellion, I remembered a discussion I had several months before with my son Sruli. I have often relied on Sruli's nature to think outside of the box, so I asked him to find an individual mentioned in the Torah (five books), who gave up his life for the sake of his beliefs. I expected him to say that Yitzchak was prepared to (the Akeida/Binding of Isaac) or that Avraham (according to the Midrash) was also prepared to (Nimrod had him thrown into a fiery furnace, but he miraculously survived). To those I would answer that I wanted someone who followed through, and in the text itself, not the Midrash; but of course he never mentioned them. Without pausing he looked me in the eye, and said: Korach.

You've go to love that.

Living the Same Day Over and Over Again

Rabbi Eliyahu Dessler, in his "Michtav M'Eliyahu," often cited the Rabbinic teaching that each day of the year we revisit the very same "energy" of that day of previous years. Every fifteenth day of Nissan, we revisit the very same energy that was available on the fifteenth of Nissan when we left Egypt

3350 years ago. There are those who teach that just as there is a particular unique energy for each day of the calendar year, there is also a unique energy for each day of the month, and then for each day of the week, and even for each part of the day.

This is a depressing message for someone who is looking for adventure, excitement, and pleasant surprise from their day. Once I've been through a few cycles and found the context of my life to be basically the same thing over and over, I start to wonder what the point is. Some people decide to fight the boredom with travel to exotic locations, or a new hobby, or a change of career; they hope that by changing the context, they will somehow defeat the boredom of a cycle repeated and repeated and repeated. What they find is that after a while, they are back in the same place they always were. It's as if that place travels with them, wherever they go, and whatever they do. They can't escape it.

The truth is the newness is not in the energy of the moment but in what I do with that energy, what I make from it. Each moment is a fresh opportunity for me to grow and fix and create; and because I have infinite potential for growth, the opportunities are limitless. As I approach each moment with new abilities, new possibilities, new powers of creation, I find newness everywhere. Its not about the context, it's about what I do. The newness is there, I've just been looking for it in the wrong place.

Watching the News

When we watch the evening news, everything we hear and see will have already happened. The news anchors are telling us stories. We watch because we believe that knowing those stories will help us navigate the path from the present to the future.

We hear the same story over and over again, told with slight variation. Books and movies are the same book or movie, made with different actors or characters, set in different settings, but the same story.

How many times do I have to listen to the same story before I absorb its lesson?

I remember reading stories to my young children. They wanted to hear the same story over and over. I would read it because I loved them, and experienced powerful joy when I pleased them; but in the back of my mind I noted how silly it was to read the same story over and over. The same happened with songs, the same song, over and over and over and over, until it became almost unbearable.

Imagine G-d's love and patience, playing the same story over and over, the same song over and over, and I continue to ask him to play it again, still not getting it.

Conquering Fear

Muhamad Ali was my hero when I was fifteen. He was supremely talented, powerful, and didn't disappoint (too often), and most important; he was fearless. I didn't have much to worry about at age fifteen, so "fearless," while important, was not worth studying. As I continued to travel down the path of my life, I began to accumulate relationships, dreams, and items, and worry introduced itself. Dealing with worry became a vocation. (Have you ever walked into a Sharpe Image or Hamacher Schlemmer and browsed? Did you notice how much shelf space is devoted to items for the relief of stress? Just thinking about a massage chair gives me goose bumps.)

I have discovered several methods for dealing with fear, and there is one I prize above all.

The first three methods are not strictly methods, they are conditions.

The first of the three, and the father of the group, is ignorance. If you don't know there is something to fear, you're not afraid. It's that simple.

The next condition is a subcategory of ignorance, arrogance. When you're arrogant you aren't afraid because in your eyes there is nothing that can defeat you; you are so much better than any opponent, what could there be to fear? Arrogance is an ignorance of the reality, caused by a distortion of perception, and is sometimes a very valuable tool when confronting a fearsome opponent. This was Muhamad Ali's, not-so-secret, weapon. (The title of his autobiography was "I am the Greatest.")

The third condition is a subcategory of arrogance, anger. If I'm angry enough, I fear nothing. Rosa Parks was angry and refused to move to the back of the bus, setting off a wave of protest that challenged the white power structure of the South. Anger generates the same distorted perception that arrogance does; you loom large, and everything else shrinks to the point where they are in danger of disappearing altogether.

My favorite method to practice, and it requires lots of practice, is simply to let go. Not to let go of my relationships or my dreams or even of my things, but to let go of my desire to control my life's various outcomes. (I have developed the insane assumption that I am somehow in control of future events, and that if I can't figure out how to manipulate things so that everything works out, disaster will happen.) Letting go, allowing G-d to run things and to continue to bestow His goodness upon me, is letting go of worry. It works, it's good, but it requires disciplined practice, which is why, most of the time, I end up settling for one of the first three.

On the Art of Communication

Communication is an art, but unlike many of the disciplines, it cannot be practiced alone. It requires the combined effort of at least two. We might call these artists, "expressionists."

Most of us assume that all we have to do is say what we think in the direction of the person with whom we want to interact, and we're done. What we discover, if we should ever stick around long enough to witness the results of our interaction, is that rarely does the other person interpret what we said in the way we meant it to be received. In fact, after a bit of investigation, we often find that we ourselves didn't have a complete grasp on what we wanted to articulate when we spoke.

Here's an example:

A teenage girl comes home from school, opens the refrigerator, takes out a plate with a piece of cake on it, and then after quickly eating the cake, leaves the plate on the kitchen table. Her mother sees the crumb filled plate on the table and yells at the daughter for not cleaning up after herself. The girl, stung by her mother's rebuke, angrily answers back, and before you know it, their exchanges have escalated into a world war.

What the girl didn't know, had no way of knowing, was that her mother, at the moment she saw the plate on the table, had been completely overwhelmed, because she believed that all of the problems of the world were resting on her shoulders, and she was afraid that she was not going able to solve them. When she saw the plate, it was a message in code, which she read as: Yes, all of the problems of the world are on your shoulders, and no one is going to help you, no one!

The mother could have told her daughter how she was feeling and why it mattered so much to her at that particular moment, and the daughter most certainly would have reacted differently; but the mother was as clueless as the daughter about the source of her anger. "Expressionists" will, after calming down, examine the scuffle together and using their shared experience and mutual respect, they will unravel the hidden messages in their respective words and get to the core of the interchange. They will then develop a short cut, so that when a similar circumstance arises, they will understand what is happening while it is happening and spare themselves the hard feelings.

After many years, these teams of "expressionists" will develop tens, perhaps hundreds of communication shortcuts and codes, which they will utilize in the fashion of a skating pair that have rehearsed their routines hundreds of times together, and who eventually skate beautifully, and apparently effortlessly, to glorious music, and the admiration of all who look upon them.

Or…the pair could develop into deep listeners, and develop sharp awareness, and apply them to their relationship… either way.

Funny Dreams

Once, in the middle of the night, I woke from a dream, laughing. Something slapstick-like had played out in my dream, and I was still laughing at it. Sometimes, when something like that happens, I try to determine if there was something genuinely funny happening, or perhaps it wasn't really that funny, but I knew I was supposed to laugh, so I did. But that night I was curious about something else; let's assume that something genuinely funny did happen. Slapstick is funny because you're not expecting it to happen. If I know the person is going to slip on the banana peel, it's not funny to watch him slip, it's boring.

I remember reading about a director who asked Charlie Chaplin's advice for a movie he was making. The director wanted to show someone slipping on a banana peel, but with a twist that would get a big laugh. Charlie Chaplin suggested he show someone walking down a street, whistling and looking around, and then have the camera focus on a banana peel, lying right in the man's path. After a moment the camera should return to the man walking, and then back to the banana peel, back to the man walking, back to the banana peel, and then follow the man as he lifts his foot and steps over the banana peel, missing it entirely, as he falls into a manhole. That's funny, because it's a surprise.

So how could I be laughing at slapstick that was happening in my dream if I was generating the image? I knew what was going to happen. I once read that Freud believed that when we dream we are everyone in the dream. If in my dream my dog, Toto, and I are being chased by a wicked witch riding a bicycle, I am me, I am Toto, I am the witch, and I am even the bicycle. When interpreting the dream, it is helpful to understand it from the perspective of each of the various characters, because they are each an expression of some inner aspect of myself. In order to pull that off in a dream, I have to be able to compartmentalize. I play each character, but I'm not consciously aware that I am doing that. I've divided myself up into parts, and each part of me is playing a different role, to such an extent, that I can surprise myself.

This train of thought led me to admit that it was not only when I was asleep that I was doing that, but even when I was awake. I used to assume that my conscious awareness was peering out from central command, somewhere inside my being and was watching over all of my interactions, responding when appropriate. Now I know that I compartmentalize, that there are many aspects of me, directing many interactions with the world around me, each unaware of the other aspects of my doing the same. That happens emotionally, intellectually and spiritually. That is how, what I have come to think of as "I," could live my life, completely unaware that higher levels of my soul were interacting with life on another plane of existence. How "I" could think at times, that "I" was just a physical being and needed to remind myself that "I" believed otherwise. Why was it a matter of belief? If "I" was a soul, why couldn't "I" know that from experience?

The truth is, there were moments when "I" experienced the world through the eyes of my soul; they were brief, and often eerie, and generally they happened in my dreams.

Dreams, you've gotta love 'em.

Life Changes

Just over thirteen years ago, my family and I moved to Chicago from Jerusalem. Our children were born in Jerusalem and had visited the States before, but only for short, family, moments. Some time after we had settled in Chicago, I was spending time with Shauli when a thought crossed my mind: He was three and a half years old when we moved. One day, without any real preparation, he was scooped up into a taxi with his family, then onto an airplane, to a life in a different country, with all new people, speaking a different language. I wondered if he wasn't traumatized by the experience, and would some day require therapy for a phobia or the like that came of one day he was "here," and the next day, without any warning, he was suddenly "there."

I now realize how silly that thought was. Life really does change every moment, and we don't control it, G-d does. It's our desire to find continuity and stability that makes it so difficult when we are forced to confront the changing reality. If we would only let go, allow G-d to scoop us up and put us in whatever taxi life has to offer; far from being traumatized, we would be so much more at ease, so much better able to adapt. That is Faith, letting life be as it is, go as it goes, and to move along with it. Children have simple faith, we must learn from them; I certainly learned about faith from Shauli.

Focusing on my Breath

David and I often meditated together. When we did my goal was to relax and focus on my breathing. It required "letting go" of ego, which had been the main challenge of the meditation.

One morning I decided to focus my attention on the place below my nose where the breath is drawn and deposited. I also decided to use the word, "Neshima (breath)" as a silent mantra during my breathing. I had noticed before that when you say that word slowly, it sounds out a breath. The intake of air is the "Nehhh" part, and the exhale is the "Sheee" part, and then you end the exhaling with; "Mahhhh." While doing this, it becomes clear that the word Neshima is Onomatopoeic.

After breathing in this fashion for some time, the mantra that was playing in my mind amplified the sound of my breathing, and it sounded like a respirator in a hospital. An ironic thought arose: here I was trying to be just my breath, and yet when someone has no brain activity and is only his breath, many consider him dead.

This led to thoughts of another irony: While I make a great effort to live fully in the moment, an Alzheimer's patient, who can only live in the moment, is considered defective.

As you can see, I am often unsuccessful at "letting go" during meditation.

Equanimity

The Oxford English Dictionary defines "equanimity" as: "the quality or condition of being undisturbed by elation, depression or agitating emotion." This word is often used to translate the Hebrew word: "Hishtavut." The Hebrew and the Latin include the word 'equal' in the root. When used in Chassidic texts, the term seems to mean that all moments deserve the same presence of mind and attention and should always be met with peace of mind.

It's such a wonderful concept, yet it is burdened with such a clumsy appellation. Latin is fine for understanding the construction of a word, but it should be left in the laboratory and something more appropriate should be picked up for the everyday expression of such a wonderful idea.

I don't have a word yet, but I envision a term which captures the expression on the face of a hyena when he is informed that unless he makes the necessary payment, his car insurance will be cancelled.

Shmoozel

Groups of animals each have their own "group noun." This is a term used to describe a collection or congregation of those animals. For instance: A 'colony' of ants, a 'culture' of bacteria, a 'herd' of cattle, a 'brood' of chickens, and a 'pack' of dogs.

Some time ago, while I was watching a large gathering of people energetically engaged in conversation outside of Shul/ Synagogue, it occurred to me that I must coin a new term to describe that unique gathering: A 'Shmoozel.' It would be used this way: Last week I saw a vast shmoozel of people gathered outside of Beth Israel

More on My Death

Another in a series of lively meditations on my impending death:

Last week I confided to my friend Steve, that my chief concern about dying from disease at a young age is not the potential suffering, the fear of what lays in wait for me afterwards, the disappointment of lost potential; it is that people will blame me for my early demise. They will conclude that I brought it about through lack of disciplined exercise, occasional cigar smoking, a diet based on Atkins which is high on fat, a casual attitude towards diagnostic testing, too much exposure to the sun, eating fish caught in Lake Michigan, overuse of a cell phone, etc.

I imagine I will die; and when the word gets out, friends will say how sad, and then add, but of course what could we have expected with the way he lived?

We live in a culture that assumes our longevity is in our own hands; and that if we die, we must have done something wrong. Death is a punishment for not vigilantly caring for and protecting life. It's not just a punishment, it's the ultimate punishment; so if I brought it about with careless living, careless living must be the worst thing a person can do.

I know we are commanded to "vigilantly protect our lives" by the Torah, but I'm not talking about the things that would fall under the Halachic guidelines of that command; I'm talking about the assumption that death is bad, and that if you died of illness under the age of one hundred, you must have done something wrong.

Death is going to happen, we are all going to die, we will die regardless of our lifestyle. How long we live is primarily a predetermined issue. I need to live with death in mind, not afraid of it, but aware of it. I also have to stop caring about what others think.

Did you hear that computer screens emit harmful radiation or something harmful? I think I heard that pregnant women are supposed to wear some kind of lead apron when in front of the screen. I wonder where I could get my hands on one of those. Until then, I could turn the screen away from me and just hope I'm typing correctly. Here let me qowiuut noqwut qwtou [qiownmf'oidulf]oiaf[oifjf[[mmf[oekmoi0-94573570978lkamf9ul flfouf0. This is not working; how about we just keep this typing in front of the computer screen business our little secret?

Making Room for G-d

Do you ever wonder why we need a Synagogue or a Temple, to serve G-d. I mean, He's everywhere; why focus our service of him on a building?

Sometimes I find myself cleaning my desk, and after a while I realize that I'm just trying to bring order to my life. It stands to reason that if I can physically act out issues that I am experiencing internally, the physical plane is an appropriate place to work on internal issues. You would think you could just take a good look inside and then play around with what you find on the inside; but it doesn't work that way. Whether you are working on anger, or depression, or humility, or generosity, you will find that the actual work will always be done on the outside.

I imagine it working like a T.V. weatherman. It looks to the television viewer as if the weatherman is standing in front of a screen with images playing across it, but he is actually standing in front of a blank, green, board. The images we see are superimposed on the board in a manner which looks as if they are actually on the board, but they are not. For the weather man it remains a blank, green, board. He watches a television monitor in front of him, and uses that as a guide for where to point. That's why T.V. weathermen always look awkward when they point to something on the board; they have to look somewhere else to see what it is they are pointing at. Our insides are equally blank for us, so we need to look at something outside of us to guide us where to point.

"And they shall make me a sanctuary and I will dwell amongst them." Shemot 25/8

The Torah should be written: "I will dwell in it." Why does it say: "I will dwell amongst them?" Some suggest it means that when we build the Mishkan/Sanctuary, the Shechina/G-d's Divine Presence will dwell within us.

The Kotzker Rebbe once asked his students: "Where is G-d?" They answered that He is everywhere. The Rebbe said that was not the answer he was looking for. He wanted them to answer: "G-d is where you let him in."

Our goal when building the Mishkan/Tabernacle, or even a synagogue, is not to have a place to worship G-d on the outside; but to open up a space within ourselves for G-d to dwell.

Miracles

I browsed through a Rabbinical Council of America Manual of Holiday and Occasional Sermons published in 1943. An article by Louis Engelberg, Chaplain in the US Army drew my attention. I guess I've been thinking a little too much about Mel Gibson's "Passion," and found the following anecdote of Rabbi Engelberg, particularly apropos:

It is told that the late General Sikorski Commander in Chief of the Polish forces asked a Rabbi in Palestine what he thought would be the outcome of the war. The Rabbi's reply was: "We shall win the war in one of two ways - either by natural means, or through a miracle."

"What," asked Sikorski, "do you consider natural means?"

The Rabbi's reply was: "Since we are fighting a just and righteous war, it is natural to expect Divine intervention – G-d's help."

Surprised, Sikorski asked: "What then would be a miracle?"

To which the Rabbi replied: "It would be a miracle if we won without Divine intervention."

Outsourcing

Last week, the administrative director at our Torah Learning Center, Ali, was speaking with someone about some bank-related issue when it became clear to her that this person was speaking to her from India. According to Forbes.com, over the next 15 years, 3.3 million U.S. services industry jobs and $136 billion will go overseas, for the most part to India and China. This can happen because telephones, faxes, and computers allow us to communicate from pretty much anywhere.

You're wondering; "How can I make use of this new context for getting things done?" Well, I've been thinking about this, and several possibilities came quickly to mind:

1. Communication. Keeping in touch with family members who live out of town. These relationships are primarily maintained over the phone or internet, and could easily be outsourced to someone with just a modicum of background information provided. In many cases, because they don't have the baggage associated with familial relationships, the surrogate might be better equipped to maintain a healthy relationship with the family members.

2. Education. It is now possible to study via the internet at almost every level, and almost any subject of interest. Why be bogged down gathering all of the information required for a degree, when you could have someone else gathering the

information for you and you could be busy doing something else? If you ever need the information, it will be only an e-mail message away.

3. Household maintenance. Bill paying, the hiring of maintenance personnel, baby sitters, house cleaners, the ordering of food and more, can all be done over the internet.

4. Civic duty. Soon we will be able to vote over the internet. Let's face it, how much time do I have to research every position on the ballot. An outsourced researcher in China could do all of the research and vote for me. He or she could also research charities and write letters of protest, letters to the editor, sign petitions and so much more.

5. Enhanced relationship with G-d, development of character, loving, giving, sharing, growing, being ... well, four out of five isn't bad.

Powerful Rivers

"A river is unlike most other landscape forms; it is less a thing than a process. Its essence is movement. A river may be old, like the Connecticut, but in another sense it is eternally young, because the flow is always being renewed, endlessly, from one second to the next. As the Greek, philosopher Heraclitus said, no man can step in the same river twice.

...Suffice it to say that a river is mysterious. It is always different and it is ever the same. It can never be fully understood. It is possible, however to build a relationship with a river, but it takes time...." (*Upstream, A Voyage on the Connecticut River*, by Ben Bachman, Published by Houghton Mifflin)

The other day I finished the book; *River Horse*, by William Least Heat Moon. What a wonderful window into the life force of rivers. Over the past several years, I have developed a travel lust, which I indulge every so often, generally on family driving trips. After driving thousands of miles on American interstates, I have experienced rivers as almost imperceptible lines, marked by bridges and signs. Even the Mississippi, which we have crossed from at least eight different points, always requires a quick; "Everybody get up and pay attention, we're crossing the Mississippi river."

I love water. I relish living near it and enjoy swimming in it. I grew up only a few blocks from Lake Michigan and continue to live not far from it. I get tremendous pleasure driving along Chicago's Lake Shore Drive. My friend David once showed me a pier you can drive onto which allows you to feel like you're driving into the lake. On windy days, when the waves swell, it's an awe filled experience. When I lived in Israel, I traveled to the Mediterranean, the Dead Sea, the Kineret, the Red Sea, whenever I could. Yet for some reason, rivers are not on my radar.

It amazes me that something so powerful, as vibrant as a river, can run by or below me, and I feel nothing. But why am I surprised, when everything said about a river could be said about the Soul, and I find myself in contact with so many of souls, without fully experiencing their vibrancy and powerful life force.

Insanity

I am teetering on the brink of insanity. If I could only follow the basic rules for the maintenance of the collective illusion projected by the rest of the people on this plane of existence, I would be O.K. My challenge is to maintain fidelity to that illusion, while challenging its most basic premises.

I am a Jew, and as a Jew I declare that something unseen, G-d, is the creator of existence, is in fact the whole of existence; and that we ourselves are essentially spirit, thinly veiled in a physical wrapping. I believe that the bestowing of goodness is at the root of the very purpose of creation. I believe that the Jewish people were singled out to model the desired relationship with G-d, and that upon the success of our tutorial, we will usher in the messianic age.

What are my chances?

Falling

Once, I lost my balance. It was not the first time, but it was the first time in a while that I fell off the wire. You know those moments when an accident has just begun, you become paralyzed into the role of an observer, and events unfold in slow motion. I had that moment then, but there was no real accident, what seemed to fall apart was just a life plan, one of those plans where "Der mensch tracht und G-tt lacht/Man thinks and G-d laughs."

This was not the first time I had become rigidly invested in a plan. My problem was that I never noticed, or refused to notice, how fixed I was on a particular outcome, until it appeared that it wouldn't work out. My recognition finally hit me in the form of panic; blood rushed to my head, and pulsed loudly through my temples. It was about that very experience that Rav Nachman of Breslov wrote: 'The entire universe is a very narrow bridge; the main thing is not to be afraid." For a long time I wondered how I can know when my fear is inappropriate. It was then, I discovered, that when my fear is inappropriate there is no room for G-d. I never think of G-d in those moments.

So there I was, one moment balancing on the high wire, my pole stretched out, held easily in my hands, the next moment falling through the air, those same hands desperately clinging to the now useless pole. Instead of onto a net, I fell into the middle of a huge body of water, which I took to be an ocean. The pole, once an aid for balance, had now become a floatation device. Once I got my bearings, I realized that the sea was a tempest and that ahead of me, rapidly approaching, were huge waves that continued to rise as they approached. It was then I remembered a story of Raba Bar Bar Chana:

"I was told by Sailors about a wave that sinks ships and has a white fire at its tip, but when struck with a club which is engraved with the three names of G-d: "I shall be as I shall be," Y-h, and "G-d of Legions" and then "Amen, Amen, Selah," it subsides."

It was time to daven/pray. The waves subsided but still remained formidable. It was then I remembered a teaching of Rabbi Akiva:

"I was once traveling on a ship," recounted Rabban Gamliel, "when I

saw that another ship was wrecked. My heart grieved, especially

for one of its passengers, the Torah Sage: Rabbi Akiva. When I reached land and resumed my studies, he approached and then sat before me to discuss halachic matters." When Rabban Gamliel asked who rescued him from the sea, Rabbi Akiva replied: "A plank from the ship came my way and I grabbed on to it; as each wave surged towards me, I bowed my head and let it pass over me."

Taking direction from Rabbi Akiva, I held on to my pole and bowed my head, and just like Rabbi Akiva's waves, mine passed over me.

I continue to swim the ocean, but I'm getting used to the waves. The truth is I like it better down here than up on the high wire; the water's cool, the fish are pleasant, and I've discovered I'm quite buoyant.

Listening with your Face

"Will you listen to me with the front of your face?" – A three-year-old's request of her mother. (Mimi Doe, Spiritualparenting.com).

After hearing this, it struck me that G-d did not just speak to Moshe "Face to Face," He paid attention. More than I want to hear what G-d has to say, I need him to listen. Is that selfish?

Spring

I don't ever remember experiencing Spring with this level of intensity. There can't be any place finer for experiencing the 'seasons' than Middle America. The changing seasons are the Rocky Mountains of Wisconsin, the Grand Canyon of Minnesota, and the Niagara Falls of Illinois.

I think what made my spring experience this year so powerful was that I allowed myself to fully experience winter. Winter is frightening, it's like death. But when I allowed myself to come to terms with death, life became more colorful, more vibrant

Dependence

This year I have been living with an idea that continues to take shape in my mind:

According to the Kabbalists, as explained in the book; "The Way of G-d," by Rabbi Moshe Chaim Luzzatto, the reason G-d created the universe is because He is Goodness, and Good must give. This means that He created us so that He could give, and because He will always need to give, we will always be receiving. We will be receiving in 'Messianic' times, after we die, and in the times of 'Ressurection of the Dead.'

I always imagined that one day I would achieve independence, self sufficiency; but now I know that was wrong, I will never be independent or self sufficient, never, not in any stage of my existence; I will always be dependent on G-d.

Gratitude for American Soldiers

Last week I had the pleasure of sharing a Pesach meal with Dr. Zeffren. At one point he turned to me and said that he thinks too many people, especially Jews, take American soldiers for granted. We Jews in particular are often so focused on Israel and its daily struggle for survival; we forget that we live in a country that is without compare, which will only remain so because of the sacrifice of soldiers like those fighting in Iraq.

There are people dying every day, so that the Jewish People can recover from the devastation of the Holocaust, so that I can teach Torah and take my kids to baseball games, so that my wife and I can live in freedom and safety, in a comfortable home, in beautiful surroundings.

For those soldiers, and those who give up time with their families and risk danger, I am grateful.

Magic

I am a magician. I have been secretly perfecting magical talents. What makes my case so unusual is that I am the one from whom the secret is being kept. Permit me to explain:

In the classic case of a magic trick, the magician practices an illusion over and over in private; and then when it has been perfected, he performs it before an unwitting audience. For him it is a series of moves wrapped in misdirection and sleight of hand; there is no mystery, no wonder; just the pleasure he receives from the reaction of his audience. For the audience it is … magic; shocking, surprising, unbelievable, magic.

My magic is the opposite. I perfect illusions, which after much practice fool only me. Anyone who is watching sees exactly what is happening and is amused only by my own surprise. This is true regarding many of my personal traits and habits. I am always beguiled and amused by them, while others are annoyed or hurt by them. This is true regarding many of my insights, I think of them as bold, unique, and important; while my mentors smile and think they're … cute.

A great magician never rests, he is always planning, devising, dreaming, for and of his next illusion. I am no different. I have a few ideas already; I just have to wait until I'm not paying attention so I can practice them … that should happen in: five, four, three, two ………….

The Physics of Suffering

My knowledge of physics comes from popular books, designed to explain its principles to the layman. My understanding is that the laws we presently identify as governing the movement of subatomic particles are different from those which govern the movement of the grand objects of the cosmos.

I find this a useful analogy for understanding the Talmudic approach to everyday suffering. The Talmud, in Tractate Brachot 5a, describes a practice for dealing with suffering:

"If a person suffers, he should examine his actions. If he doesn't find a suitable explanation, he should attribute the difficulties to not learning Torah when he has the opportunity. If he doesn't find that this could be the cause, he knows it is "yesurim shel ahava/ suffering caused by G-d's love of us."

In practice, whenever you feel pain, you examine your actions. When you find something which explains the suffering, you devote yourself to repairing it and then move on. The theology at work here is that G-d responds to our behavior measure for measure, so that we can identify our incorrect actions and then fix them. He wants us to learn from our suffering and expects us to understand it. I have found it to be a very useful practice.

There are some who find this practice frightening because it assumes that suffering is caused by incorrect action or as part of some kind of demonstration of G-d's love. This means that the people who died in the Holocaust must have done something wrong. This is when I draw upon the physics analogy. I am comfortable applying the Talmudic teaching in the 'micro' world of my own manageable suffering, while at the same time understanding that the laws upon which I rely in my private life, do not satisfactorily explain the 'macro' suffering of others.

Living in Denial

Rav Asher Rubinstein, the Mashgiach Ruchani/Spiritual Mentor at Yeshivas Mishkan Hatorah, used to give fiery Shmoozen/lectures, on ethics. It was not his delivery as much as his rhetoric that was so frightening. He gave them on Thursday nights, and generally the students would gather and talk about them afterwards. Older guys, veterans of the Thursday night Shmoozen, would often go over to younger guys, afraid that if they didn't say a quick few words of comfort, the new guys would be traumatized. He held nothing back.

Truth be told, the lectures were not just fire and brimstone, they often included thoughtful insights into the psychology of the individual. I remember one in particular: He was talking to us about the ills caused by exposure to the values of corrupt cultures. One of his consistent subjects was the inevitable pollution of the soul that would come from reading popular newspapers and magazines. Forget, for a moment, the lurid pictures and detailed descriptions of every form of immoral lifestyle; just the exposure to lies on a consistent basis was harmful.

Whenever we read a *Time* or *Newsweek* article about Israel, we would be incensed at the lies and misrepresentations. Why, he asked, did we assume that it was only about Israel they were lying? We should extrapolate from what we knew to be true in the case of Israel, and assume that they were lying about everything else. Yet we didn't. We blissfully soaked up every detail of what was said on every other subject as if it were G-d's truth. Why? Because we didn't know enough about anything else to tell that they were lying, and we didn't care.

I think of that often as I read something on the internet or in a newspaper, and then quickly repress it, and read on.

Killing Your Self

A young man once spoke at my shabbos table. He was drunk, very, very, drunk. He began to speak about his pain. He was, he said, in emotional pain every day, and he was tired of his pain. If only he would kill himself, then his pain would be over. As he was talking, it struck me that he was right, his pain would not end until he killed his self.

There are several ways a person can kill his "self:" 1. He can actually, physically, end his life. 2. He can obliterate his "self" through drug and alcohol use. 3. He can escape his self by becoming completely absorbed in an "other." 4. He can become humble and nullify his "self."

Many of the humblest people I have met knew great suffering. Maybe their suffering fueled their path to humility.

The Sound of Silence

There is nothing more filled with sound than quiet. It is fascinating to listen to the cacophony of my internal sounds, if not a bit frightening. After all, who knows what I might hear.

My personal, layman's approach to quiet has always been to make so much external noise that I can't hear the sounds from within. This is tiring and uses up a certain degree of time and ingenuity. A more direct and more conservationist approach, would be to quiet the sounds from within. I have learned that this can be accomplished by giving them a chance to be heard. When I pause and pay attention to the sounds, they say their piece, hover for a moment, and then disappear in a wisp.

What are those sounds, and where do they come from? There can't be a voice without a speaker. Just how many of me are there? They might be inventions, but then who invented them?

Who is asking?

Yes, "Who" is asking?

Costello: I mean the fellow's name.

Abbott: Who.

Costello: The guy who's asking.

Abbott: Who.

Costello: The guy with the question.

Abbott: Who.

Costello: The guy asking...

Abbott: Who is asking!

Costello: I'm asking YOU who's asking.

Abbott: That's the man's name.

Costello: That's who's name?

Abbott: Yes.

Costello: Well go ahead and tell me.

Abbott: That's it.

Costello: That's who?

Abbott: Yes.

The Invisible Man

In this week's Torah portion, Aharon is charged with lighting the Menorah. The mystics suggest that the light of the Menorah represents the light of Torah, the light of the wisdom it contains. Aharon is humility, that's why he could be the invisible conduit between man and G-d, and that is why he lights the Menorah because only a humble person can stand in front of the light and not diminish it.

Developing My Psychic Powers

I am working on developing my psychic powers. The field is a crowded one, every city has dozens of psychics offering their services at ten dollars a pop, but I have an angle. Psychics make their bread and butter telling people about their pasts and futures. I will be different; I will develop my senses until they are strings on the finely tuned instrument of my spirit, and then gaze deeply into the ... present.

Retreats

I was reading an article by Amy Cunningham called "Summery Ways to Spiritually Expand," which was featured on Beliefnet. She suggested that one of the spiritual options available for the summer was a summer retreat. She provided a link to retreat sites all over the country.

I checked out Illinois, and found forty-nine centers listed, all but one of them, Christian. My first reaction was disappointment; why didn't Judaism stress retreat to the extent that Christianity and Buddhism did? But then I understood, the Torah stressed living within community and immersing oneself in everyday life. The Torah implied that the Nazir who separated himself from community was not to be considered the ideal, but a necessary evil. That is why, while the Jewish calendar and Jewish community have always provided brief opportunities for retreat, retreat centers have never been a priority.

We can't do it Alone

I once put up a tent in our back yard. I was practicing for a road trip my family would be taking. I did it alone because my boys were visiting with their cousins in St. Louis and my wife was busy at work. I was able to put up the tent but I couldn't get the rain cover up without someone else to help. There it sat awaiting the return of my boys.

Later, I went fishing. I had a small inflatable Zodiac type boat. I inflated the boat with an electric pump, loaded it with my rod and tackle and a cooler with some diet coke. The water was significantly shallower in the Skokie lagoons than in previous years, which made getting the boat on the water more of an effort. By the time I was rowing on open water I was exhausted. It was the first time I had used the boat alone.

My boys are growing, and my wife and I will have more time to ourselves; that day I was reminded that life was not meant to be lived alone. (Even after some pleading, my wife has assured me that she won't be joining me on fishing expeditions any time soon; although she might help with the tent.)

The 'Three Weeks' is a time for reflection on the destruction of the two Temples, and why it is that we haven't been able to get our act together since then. The Talmud suggests that the 2nd Temple was destroyed by unwarranted hatred. That hatred is with us today.

Maybe we would feel more motivated to do something about the hatred if we felt we needed each other. We have come to the mistaken conclusion that each of our little groups can do it all on our own. But take a good look around you, isn't it obvious that we can't?

Sweet Suffering

At the Major League Baseball All-Star game in 1999, Ted Williams threw out the first ball. Before he did that, he chatted with some of the players, one of whom was Mark McGwire.

"...Afterward Williams recounted what he said:

"They wanted me to meet [Don] Mattingly when he was going good, and [Wade] Boggs. And we went to this high-class restaurant and we're talking about hitting, the intimate part of hitting, where you put your foot, everything like that. Finally, I said, 'Did you guys ever smell the wood when you foul one real hard?'

"They looked at one another, like what's this guy smoking now? And I said I could smell it quite a few times, and it smelled like wood burning. I said the next time I see Willie Mays, the next time I see Cepeda, the next time I see Reggie Jackson, I'm going to ask them.

They said, 'Oh, sure, we've smelled it, too.' So I asked McGwire the same thing, and he said he could smell it, too."

(CNN/SI, posted: Wednesday July 14, 1999 02:48 AM)

I've had a similar experience. There were several times when cataclysmic events happened in my life, often apparently tragic. During those moments, I noticed a sweetness, which I experienced as the palpable closeness of G-d. I couldn't help myself; I had to know if other people had the same experience. More than once, I asked someone who had just suffered a tragedy, if they felt that sweetness. Several looked at me deeply, and said; yes they did.

Is Life a Particle or a Wave?

There is a part of me that wants life to stand still, to remain the same. I remember a lecture given by Rabbi Mendel Weinbach at Ohr Somayach when he asked: If you could press a button and freeze your life at any moment, which moment would it be?

I used to think of life as a particle, not a wave. As a particle, my life traveled through time, a defined unit, and could be stopped by the button Rabbi Weinbach imagined. It existed entirely in the present and was self contained. The question was whether I wanted to take an experience I already had and make it my life forever, or gamble on there being an even more meaningful moment to freeze in the future.

Now I think of life as a wave. This wave is made up of my life and experiences, as well as the lives and experiences of everyone else. It is made up not just of the lives of everyone, but by everything, alive or not, and most especially, G-d. This wave moves in the medium of time, but it not only rolls through the present, it is, simultaneously, in the past, present, and future. Life as a wave, is continuously moving, always changing; change and movement are necessary conditions for such a life.

This has something to do with the World to Come, which according to Rabbi Chaim of Volozhin (Nefesh Hachaim), is more properly translated: the World that Comes ... (of our lives/experiences/actions).

Happiness

The other day I was teaching a class about happiness. The question put before the group was whether the Torah considers our happiness an important goal. In the course of the discussion, Steve made a wonderful observation: We want our parents to be proud and therefore pursue uncomfortable and sometimes painful paths to make them proud; and we want our children to be happy which means not being uncomfortable and in pain. That combination leads many of us to make life decisions we don't want our children to emulate.

Eating and Drinking Prayer

One of the primary purposes of organized Tefillah/Prayer is to help me on a soulful journey. My consciousness must travel inward; leave the plane of the material to a place that is a higher aspect of my soul. It is in that place that it will make contact with G-d. I will then cleave to G-d for as long as it is reasonable.

This is not just something I can do, it is something I need to do, not unlike my need for food and water. I need to eat and drink in order to nourish my body. Lately, I have thought of eating and drinking as models for two modes of Tefillah, the spontaneous and the composed.

Eating requires preparation, drinking does not. Drinking Tefillah is simple and spontaneous, when I'm thirsty; I drink until my thirst is slaked. Eating Tefillah, on the other hand, is a planned event that happens at a certain time and is composed.

The food is selected, prepared, cooked; and then with some degree of formality, it is eaten. My own personal experience with heartburn has taught me that the meal is best eaten calmly and with attention.

I like the metaphor, but it could be interpreted as a bit 'self'ish. Eating is often experienced as self gratification, and Tefillah will ultimately not be healthy, if it is only a matter of self gratification. In order to keep it from being 'all about me,' I have to have a focus that is beyond me, I have to focus on G-d and the greater good of humanity. This is why the composed prayers are in the plural, and emphasize my role as a servant to help keep me humble.

Eating and drinking don't have to be just about gratification either. We can eat and drink because G-d wants us to guard our health, and we can share our food and drink with others. Maybe that's why hospitality is considered bedrock of Jewish practice. It helps us direct otherwise selfish needs outside of ourselves.

I Love You

My favorite explanation for the etymology of Bracha, Hebrew for blessing, is that given by the Rashba (Rabbi Shlomo Ben Aderet 1300 ce). He said that the word Bracha is related to the word Breicha, which means a pool of water, and that blessing was Divine energy which we send to someone else, like water sent from a pool to irrigate a field. That water provides the energy necessary to bring out the potential in the seed, and blessing provides the energy necessary to bring out the positive potential in the person.

A modern day equivalent to blessing is "I love you." When I say; "I love you," I'm not just telling you a fact, I'm sending you my love. That love travels from me to you and then it unfolds inside of you, enlivening you, energizing you and unleashing waves of potential with in you.

Experiment: Wait for a quiet moment and tell your spouse, child, parent, sibling, friend, that you love him or her. Watch the person's face as it glows with that love.

That is Bracha.

The Doorman at the Threshold to G-d's Mind.

Jaques Derrida recently passed away. Derrida's name has become synonymous with the philosophical school of deconstruction, a mode of analysis based on the critical reading of texts.

I know next to nothing about him, and would not even know his name, if it weren't for comments made by Rabbi Cardozo and Lois the other day. Lois and Rabbi Cardozo are mentors of mine; and when they mention someone, I feel immediately compelled to study that person. I've only begun my study, and something struck me. What follows is not a teaching of Derrida, but a result of the thought process begun while studying him.

Rashi writes in his commentary on the Torah: "I have come only for the plain meaning of the text, and Midrash which resolves matters of the text..." You would think that Rashi's commentary would be considered a primer, once studied and then left behind. But history has shown that rather than a mere discussion of simple meanings, Rashi's commentary has become the doorway to the most profound ideas of G-d and existence. It is precisely his insistence on understanding the plain meaning of the text which allows us entrée into the deepest realm of Torah. Derrida is famous for asserting: "There is nothing outside the text."

We are taught that Torah can be understood on four planes, Pshat Remez, Drush, and Sod. They are generally summed up to mean the plain meaning of the text, the meaning hinted at in the text, the more intuitive reading of the text, and the kabbalistic reading of the text. An acronym, PRDS, which means Paradise or an Orchard, is often used to represent these four levels.

Until today I imagined PRDS to be an iceberg, with the Pshat above water, the Remez just below the surface, the Midrash in the just barely visible depths, and finally the hidden, mysterious Sod. Today I've begun to think of them as a pyramid.

The difference between an iceberg and a pyramid as metaphors is subtle, but I think dramatic. The context of the iceberg is the water, and our attention is focused on the surface of that water. In that context Pshat is the focus of our attention, Sod is simply a hidden mystery, way below in the depths. But the pyramid is built on land. The focus of our attention on land is its surface. With the pyramid, Sod is prominent as the foundation upon which everything else stands.

Why do I care so much about my choice of metaphor? I care because I think it helps clarify the path of Torah study and that the goal requires travel beyond the realm of Pshat. I began to study Torah because I was supposed to. That is what I was taught since I was a child. The first teaching a child hears: "Torah Tziva Lanu Moshe (Moshe commanded us Torah) Morasha Kehilas Yaakov (As an inheritance of the Congregation of Yaakov)." Torah is our unique heritage, and we must study it in order to know how to practice, and in order to pass it on to our children.

It wasn't until I was in my young twenties that I began to realize that Torah is the context for embracing G-d and that what I wanted, more than anything, was to be in His embrace, to be hugged by G-d. That by connecting to the Torah, I could connect to G-d.

This is where some of the Derrida discussion got me thinking. One of the most dramatic practices of his deconstuctionist philosophy was challenging our assumptions as to what comes first, what is prior. He challenged the notion that speech comes before writing, for instance. If we apply this practice to the hierarchy of planes of Torah understanding, a shift occurs. I begin with my assertion that Torah is G-d's communication with me. If I want to achieve intimate embrace with G-d via Torah, then I have to begin with the plain meaning of the text in order to get back to the original thought. Pshat is only the beginning of study; it is not truly 'first.' It is merely meant to lead me somewhere else; that somewhere else is the more fundamental, the more important, really the beginning. (This conclusion about what is 'prior,' would be challenged by Derrida, but that's another discussion).

There is a mystical model that is often used to explain four planes of the universe. They are Atzilut, Briya, Yetzirah and Assiyah, often translated as Emanation, Creation, Formation, and Action. I once heard the following explanation for these four planes of existence. Imagine that you are attending a play. During intermission you begin thinking about how impressed you are with it, but who, you wonder, deserves the credit for it? There are the actors, the director, the writer, and whoever first conceived the idea. That's how everything comes into existence. First there is an idea, it has no form per se, and then it is fleshed out, given definition, and then form, and finally it is given body. With a play there is whoever came up with the idea (most likely the writer), and then the writer and directors who combine to give it form, and finally the actors who give it body. Everything comes into being in that way. Atzilut is the first level out of which an idea emerges into the next level, which is Briyah, and then it is given form in Yetzira, and finally body in Assiya. If we use our pyramid of the four levels of Torah, Sod would be at the birth of the idea, and Pshat would be the idea given body.

The original thought is in G-d's mind, so to speak. If I can get there, I will have the closeness I desire. Pshat is then the first step towards that goal, it's where I must start, and then work my way backwards. The foundation of the idea is the Sod. The realm beyond Sod is my goal.

Although we have come to the conclusion that Pshat is not 'first,' that doesn't mean it is not important. It is after all the doorway to G-d's mind. And when Rashi asserts that he comes to explain Pshat, he introduces himself to us as the doorman, at the threshold to G-d's mind.

G-d Protects the Fools

On my tombstone, I want only one phrase carved; "G-d protects the fools... (Tehillim/Psalms, 116/6)." I think that one phrase most succinctly captures the texture and quality of my life.

There is another teaching which I've considered because it too captures much of my experience:

Man is led along the path he wishes to walk. (Talmud Tractate Makot, 10b)"

This is usually understood to mean that a person can choose his path and will receive Divine help. Even if he should choose a destructive path, he will be led along the path of his choosing.

Lately, I've experienced another possible meaning to that teaching, that G-d allows me to do things my way. He does this, even though I am surrounded by people who can do everything that I do better than I can do it. And that being the case, I should, if I could, ask them to give me direction regarding everything I do. I'm certain that if I did, regarding most things, they would give me advice to do differently than I am doing. So why don't I ask them?

Sure, every once in a while there is something that no one can help me with, something only I truly understand because of some unique predicament or perspective; but those are rare. Most of the actions I take are relatively routine, are the same as ones taken by many people who could certainly help me do things in the best way possible.

I believe the culprit is my 'I,' which insists on expressing its unique 'self' and is deluded into believing that the expression of such uniqueness requires very little asking of direction. This is a quality that I share with most of the male humans on this planet. (I am typing this quickly because as chance would have it, my I is not paying attention at this moment… must finish before 'it' comes back)

It was while pondering this predicament that I saw the above teaching in a different light: that G-d allows us to walk in our own path, allows us to achieve our purpose, to find our goal, even if because of conceit, our path is not the most efficient or appropriate.

How did I choose one epitaph over the other? Simple, I found a tombstone on e-bay with the phrase from Tehillim, and so far, I'm the only bidder.

The Joy of Downsizing

I imagine a man in his fifties, sitting at an impressive desk, in an impressive office, at the top of an impressive building. He is well coiffed, his suit is well tailored, his nails manicured. His rival, an equally well stationed, well coiffed, gentleman, from an equally well appointed office enters our man's office, and with an expression of glee, hands our man a memo.

The memo states, that because of a successful, hostile, action, taken by the rival, our man no longer works for his firm. Our man contemplates his circumstances for a moment. He has enjoyed every moment of the time he worked for the firm, enjoyed all of the trappings of his success. He scans his office, no more desk, no more view, no more deference from thousands of underlings. He won't be able to afford clothing of the likes he has become accustomed, will have to give up his club membership, will loose the chauffeur, and trips via private jet. He looks up at his rival, smiles and says, "Yes!" with enthusiasm. "This is truly a great day!" he adds, and then opening a cedar humidor on his desk, he withdraws two Cuban cigars, offering one of them to his rival, "Let's celebrate with one last cigar."

I was studying with Shmuel. We were learning from a Letter written by Rabbi Eliyahu Dessler z'l, about "vessels" and "tools" for serving G-d. Some of these "vessels" and "tools" might include talents and skills or material abundance. In the letter, Rabbi Dessler makes the point that there might be a person who is given material wealth because he needs the wealth in order to serve G-d; but then, after some time the person might grow to where he no longer needs the wealth in order to serve G-d. When that happens, the wealth is taken away. For that person, loosing the wealth is a sign he has graduated to a higher level of service.

Who wants to celebrate!

Holiness in Time

We consider Shabbat and the Holidays holiness in time. They are opportunities to commune with the most sublime energies of the universe, the very energies of creation and the exodus from Egypt and the receiving of the Torah; and yet while we do spend a portion of those days in prayer and study, a key component of each is a festive meal and pleasant recreation. The Dubner Maggid once told a parable to explain the indulgence in the physical on such holy days: Two men lived alone in separate cabins in the woods. One was lame and spent his days shut up in him home. The other was blind and deaf and spent his days shut up in his home, unaware of the world outside. One day the lame man had an idea: If he could drag himself over to the cabin of the deaf and blind man and somehow communicate that he should put him on his shoulders; then both of them could walk in the woods. The lame man dragged himself over to the home of the blind and deaf man, and before long the blind and deaf man had him on his shoulders. With the direction of the lame man and the legs of the deaf and blind man, they were soon walking in the woods. The wind blew on their cheeks, the pungent odors of the woods filled their nostrils, and the sun warmed them. They were both thrilled. As they continued on their walk, the lame man began to hear the soft notes of music being played at an inn off in the distance. He was enthralled; his joy increasing as they approached the inn and the music became louder and sharper. He wanted to stop and take in the music, but how could he communicate that to the blind and deaf man. Then he remembered. In his pocket he had a flask of whiskey. He quickly unscrewed the cap, poured some whiskey into it, and gave some to his carrier. The blind and deaf man drank, and while they were stopped, the lame man listened to the music. But the drink was quickly emptied, and the blind and deaf man wanted to continue; so the lame man poured him another drink, and then another and another. The lame man continued to listen to the music from the inn. It was exquisite. Suddenly he felt movement below him. The blind and deaf man was drunk, so drunk he began to dance. Now, not only were they listening to the music, they were dancing. The body doesn't appreciate the spiritual music that is playing on Shabbat and the Holidays, only the soul does; but if the body doesn't rest, how can the soul enjoy the music? So we fill the body with food and drink and when the clamoring of its needs quiets, not only can the soul listen to the music, it can dance to it.

Conspicuous Consumption

I am told that in order to contribute to the health of our nation's economy, I must spend money. I must buy things, preferably new cars and houses. If I or my neighbor should for any reason stop buying things, our economy will collapse. We will sink like the Titanic, drawn to the depths of the ocean of poverty, despair, and old, used, things.

I have, more than once, imagined going on a spending fast, only spending money on the barest maintenance of my lifestyle. I would buy nothing new, not attend movies, plays or sporting events. I wouldn't eat out at restaurants or order from catalogues. I would live like that for a while, just simplify and detach somewhat from things, from the frenzy of acquiring stuff.

Of course, if I ever should go on a spending fast, I wouldn't be able to tell anyone. If they found out they would hate me; at the very least I would lose lots of friends. Friends like the owners of the restaurants I frequent, the advertisers in the newspapers and magazines that I read, store owners, telemarketers, the village fathers, state and county government, the federal government, even my own President. If they found out they would consider me a traitor, a loafer, a danger, and worst of all ... not worth their time. For many of them the desirability of engaging my attention is directly related to the likelihood that I might buy something.

On the other hand, if I owned less and needed less, life would be simpler. I would worry less, I would spend more time and energy on things I truly valued and with people I genuinely cherished. At the beginning of this week's Torah Portion, Noach is described as Tamim, often translated as whole or pure, but it can also mean simple. In our culture simple is often used as a term of disrespect, but in the Torah it is high praise. Simple focus on one thing is very powerful (The man built an Ark!). Instead of allowing your limited energy to be spread over many things, each of them done with minimum efficiency, you focus on just a few things which you value above all else, and suddenly they are done well and with a flourish.

So that's it I guess, it all boils down to simple goodness or patriotism, making valuable use of my time and energy, or collecting things ...oops gotta go, my PDA's alarm just rang, to remind me that there's a sale at Hammacher Schlemmer. If I don't get there ASAP, I will miss my chance to buy a robotic vacuum cleaner with a state of the art GPS to help it navigate the various piles of things I haven't opened or even remember owning.

Know When to Hold 'Em and Know When to Fold 'Em

Eric and Gary once asked me, if I had one hundred to one odds in my favor, would I bet my entire net worth on a game? I thought about it for a moment, and said no. They told me that if I had answered yes, I would be a 'gambler,' if I answered no, then I would not. They did not define the term; 'gambler.'

Since then, I've thought about it; and like most things, I don't think it's that simple: There are some people who go out of their way to gamble, who will risk what they have, merely for the buzz; they are 'compulsive gamblers.' There are some who are just plain good at it and enjoy the competition. They may gamble for a living, but they rely on skill and an assessment of risk; they are the 'professional gamblers.' I'm sure there are many who are somewhere in between those two or both.

But there is a third category: Those who have been thrust into the game, and are forced to play, against their will. Many times in life we are faced with just such a scenario. An opponent materializes, the stakes have been set, both are holding cards, and only one of can win.

The sages have identified our "opponent" as the Yetzer Harah/Evil Inclination. They teach that all of growth requires overcoming the Yetzer Harah's plans for our failure. Succeeding at a diet, battling addictions, and withholding gossip, are just some of the challenges that pit us against "the opponent." Knowing the ways of the opponent is considered essential for victory over him. No limit, Texas Holdem, Poker, has become all the rage. Many will tell you that winning at Texas Hold'em is not luck, it's a skill; and the skill is not knowing the best hand, it's knowing your opponent. If you can read your opponent while remaining mysterious yourself, you will often win. Sun Tsu in his "Art of War" writes: "All warfare is based on deception. Hence when able to attack, we must seem unable; when using our forces, we must seem inactive; when we are near, we must make the enemy believe we are far away; when far away, we must make him believe we are near. Hold out bait to entice the enemy. Feign disorder, and crush him. If he is secure at all points, be prepared for him. If he is in superior strength, evade him." No matter who our opponents are, they are not invincible, we can always overcome. We just need to learn when to hold 'em, and when to fold 'em; and then pray a lot; lots and lots and lots of prayer.

The Candy Man

There was no one as frightening as the man who sat in the farthest back row of the synagogue. To most adults he was friendly and harmless, but we children knew better. We approached him with great care and trepidation. He never looked you straight in the eye, but he knew you were there. He was like a fisherman patiently waiting to reel you in. He did none of the work; we were lured by our own unbridled desire.

Your first time, you were led by the hand by an older, more experienced boy. He would take you to an unmarked boundary, beyond which point only one child could approach at a time. He was a mountain approached with awe. Once you were close enough, somehow you knew you were close enough, you stopped. He never changed his severe expression as he slowly reached beneath his tallit into his suit pocket. Out would come one piece of candy in a cellophane wrapper. He would hold it out for you to take, but make you tug on it to release it from his grasp. Your heart pounded so loudly you had trouble hearing your mumbled thank you, and you quickly left. No candy tasted sweeter. It was spiced with the thrill of having narrowly escaped with your life.

He was the 'Candy Man.' Candy men can be found in synagogues throughout the world and in the memories of many Jewish adults. They come in all shapes and sizes. They come from every background. There isn't a special curriculum of study, no special degree required. They represent a wide variety of professions and vocations.

The candy is usually the hard, sour, sugary, sucking kind; but they've been known to carry chewy, tangy, fruity, and even sugarless. There are even some, who afflicted with guilt about promoting ill health and tooth decay, proffer small sandwich bags, tied with twisties, containing raisins and other dried fruit. Many candy men keep their candy in a tallit bag or in their suit pocket. There was one I knew when I was young who had a secret hiding place in the synagogue. The other children and I would hide and try to spy the secret location, like stowaways on a pirate ship, who having followed the captain and his crew, hide among the trees, watching, as the captain and his trusted mates dig up their hidden treasure. The pirates buried diamonds, gold, and silver. The candy man hid sticks of gum and hard candy.

One of my great disappointments with Sigmund Freud was his omission of any mention of the candy man when discussing the stages of human development. For the Jewish boy, his candy man experience may have been the single most important developmental factor in his life. In a showdown between the candy man and a Bar Mitzvah, the Bar Mitzvah pales as a test of a young man's courage and fortitude.

I'm now passed the age when I get candy from the candy man, but I've never stopped being fascinated by him. When I go to a synagogue, I always make sure to identify the candy man and vicariously relive the experience with every child who approaches him.

Perhaps the most wonderful, vicarious, candy man experience I've had, happened in Jerusalem at a small local synagogue. The candy man of that particular synagogue survived four years in Auschwitz. He rarely smiled. It happened that on one Shabbat morning, the candy man was the chazzan and was leading the repetition of the Amidah prayer. This is a very intense moment of prayer for the chazzan, and he is not supposed to be interrupted. Even a mild mannered person would react sternly to someone who interrupted him during the repetition. On that particular Shabbat, a young boy of four or five began his approach to the candy man. Horror gripped me: someone stop that boy, was all that I could think. How could he survive the dreaded combination of the candy man and the stern rebuke for interrupting the chazan during the 'Repetition.' I thought to stop him, but I couldn't. It was his coming of age. He had to experience it alone if he was to develop into a healthy Jewish boy. One part of me wanted to look away, but I couldn't. I continued to watch with dread as the boy approached. He stopped behind the candy man, just close enough, and tugged on the woolen tallit that hung to his feet. There were no fireworks. Instead, without missing a beat, without ever turning around, the candy man reached into his suit pocket and removed a piece of candy, wrapped in cellophane, and held it behind him for the boy to take. The boy reached for the candy, and for one wonderful moment, they both tugged.

Four years in Auschwitz and yet he stood majestically before the congregation, leading them in prayer; and all the while, his worn hand and the fresh little hand of a future Jewish man, tugged at the candy, engaged in the timeless ritual of the Jewish boy's coming of age.

Wow!

You know those books with pictures that at first seem to be just blotches of color, but when you stare at them for a while, a three dimensional image pops out at you? My friend, Harlan, once suggested those as a metaphor, to help understand what its like to experience the deeper aspect of Torah.

Imagine that you are working on understanding a line, or story, from the Torah; you learn some of the commentaries, then go back to the Torah, maybe look at some more commentaries, contemplate for a while, and then, bam! It's three dimensional and in color.

Poetry

Lessons Learned from a Woodpecker

Today as I walked to work

the sky blue

the wind brisk

thin layers of ice covered recently formed puddle ponds

on lawns of greening grass

I looked up and spied a woodpecker

at first it was a woodpecker

then it was a pair of woodpeckers

pecking

nibbling

hopping along the upper reaches of a tree's trunk

how funny to consider

that the woodpecker's life is lived parallel to the tree's trunk

his up and down

our east and west

our north and south

but then consider that we live on a globe

so to someone watching from Outer Space

our down is the direction of the earth

and our up is out

that someone

watching

is only in Outer Space

because we are here

as far as he is concerned

he is here

in Inner Space

and we are there

the Sages say we live in an upside down world

the teacher is the student

and the student the teacher

in the World of Truth

Purim is when events were turned on themselves

what looked up became down

and what was down became up

upside down

was turned

upside down

and Pesach must always follow Purim

so we can be absolutely sure

that the lessons of

Pesach are learned

right side up

Back Home

I

am back

home

It

was my intent

to be

front home

with

eyes open

canvassing

dramatic vistas

available

always

but

I got so caught up

in the moments

of spectacular

places

in far away spaces

I

forgot my plan

so

here I am

back home

Yehoshua Karsh

vaguely

aware

of wonders

calling

to me

from

just outside

my

hearing

Shabbat Candles

(to be read from the bottom upwards)

air

the

in

currents

along

riding their chariots

whispered by angels

to a rhythm

slowly

blue

orange

yellow

dancing

peace

comfort

protection

joy

quiet

radiating

ivory

gold

yellows

soft

glowing

mist

smoky

hot

a

through

seen

distances

distorted

of

waves

undulating

warmth

fire

Catching Lox

Fishing lake michigan

on a chartered boat

salmon

dance on the ends

of lines

amidst

the wake

left by

powerful

engines

rods bend

worn

by years

of battling

the life force

of creatures

in the final

desperate

throes

of a game

they are

destined to

lose

I turn

to the

captain

of the craft

a lanky

weathered

ruddy

cheeked

Gentile

of a

Yehoshua Karsh

man

and

inform

him that

he is witnessing

a moment

of cosmic karma

as

I

a Jew

reel in

a giant

chunk of

lox

at that

moment

the ancient

waters of

the great lakes

and

three thousand

eight hundred

years of Jewish

history

are

one

Doing

What does my doing do

it does what it does

why do I care

I care because I do

if I didn't I wouldn't

Ach …who am I kidding

I just do that's all

if I didn't do

I wouldn't be

and if I wasn't

who would care

yes

yes

I know

that's not strictly true

I am because

He wants me to be

I do because He wants me to do

and He cares

but sometimes

I feel like

shouting

I really do

do do do do

be be be be

do be

be do

do be do be do

Yehoshua Karsh

Trying

Sometimes I try too hard

and I have nothing

if I would only stop trying

I would see I am already there

yes, yes, yes …

it can be trying

trying not to try all the time

but try as I may

I just can't stop

Camping

I awoke to the sharp staccato echoes

of birds chirping

and the first light of day

bullfrogs brayed

from amidst thickets of tall grass

that stood guard astride the pond

covered in wisps of fog

woodpeckers tapped

at one point a bird called:

yiawww, yiawww, yiawww

and then a woodpecker tapped

a masterful truah

a natural shofar delivering a greeting to the new day

a train sounded its horn in the distance

it must have been a freight train

as its horn sounded for some time

the firewood smoked

still moist from the dew

of early morning

it began to show flames

first stirrings wafted from the other tents

a baby cried

its parents cooing softly

to calm it.

A.Y. slept peacefully in our tent

Nachas

such a beautiful word

even if it sounds like a noise

you should only make

into a handkerchief

there is nothing more pleasurable for me

than to watch my father having nachas

you would think

I would only feel that

for nachas created by me

but it is not so

and I know that

because on our family camping trip

I watched my father schep nachas continuously

from his grandchildren

and I felt the same pleasure

I feel

when I am the source of his

Nachas

Decision Makers

Decision makers

are the people

who finally shape our lives

after

who knows

how much discussion

or sometimes none at all

they decide

and the parameters of our lives become fixed

yes

I can choose whether to follow

their decisions

and there are times

when I choose not to

but for the most part

I make room for them

by moving this and that

all results of earlier decisions

by people

I hardly care to know

if I were to become a decision maker

I would choose to be the one

in charge of snow days

what power he has

to bestow such expansive joy

I would consult mathematicians

and sociologists

and psychologists

and neurologists

and together

we would figure

how many snow days

can be had

in a single winter

before snow days

lose their charm

I hope they are many

and then I wonder

if I longed for Moshiach

like I long for snow days

would he come any faster

Shallots

Our main courses arrived

Tzippy and A.Y. ordered rib steaks

well done

I

a hamburger

medium rare

We ate our meat quickly

even though we had layered our stomachs

with bread and soup

for half an hour

We shared our sadness

that members of P.E.T.A

will never know the pleasure

of perfectly prepared meat

and a side of fried onions

a man at the next table snapped at the manager

he had asked for his check

twice

already

childhood friends

ate with their wives

a few tables away

whenever I see them

wonderful memories rise within me

I try to share that with them

but it always comes out lame

at another table

a man who doesn't like me

smiles and says hello

we share our best moments in restaurants

he and I

there

his feelings

probably rise within him

but then

wonderfully

magically

they cannot be shared

Baruch's Bar-Mitzvah

They say

tomorrow

it will

snow

seven inches

I consult my

schedule

if I move that

to there

and cancel

those

then maybe we can

leave earlier

eventually

white powder

will fall

on black asphalt

muffling otherwise

harsh sounds

but for now

garbage trucks

fitted with giant shovels

trail sparks

as they scrape

and bounce

on scarred pavement

when it falls

it spills

from the sky

like gobs of milky paint

it sticks to tree branches

and gathers on lawns

in piles of

perfect for snowballs

luminescent

chrystaline

powder

The sky just after sunrise

is pale blue

the snow

glows

pastel pink

It is Baruch's bar mitzvah

and family

gathers

at tables

surrounded by

ice frosted windows

eating man-quiche

and chullent

drinking Drambuie

and diet Mountain Dew

All the while

Baruch smiles

his cheeks

red with pride

reliving jokes well told

while his father

Zaide

Chananya

and his uncles

speak Torah

sections of a quilt

expertly assembled

by loved ones

wise to the ways of preserving

love and warmth

Yehoshua Karsh

Aliens

Whenever I hear people

speak of illegal aliens

I imagine

actual aliens from

outer space

If

aliens from outer space

were

reflected in a mirror

they would be

friends

of

inner

non

space

(a context for non things)

154

Friendship

exists in non space

it's a non thing

that does battle

with separation

always striving

for no distance

no duality

no otherness

Of Birds and Wannabees

Several weeks ago

when the birds first

began to return to Northbrook

I walked to work

with my binoculars

I bought them several yeas ago

in Springfield

during a stretching break

while on our way to St. Louis

I remember once hearing an artist

answer a question about art critics

whether he paid attention to them

he said he didn't

and then asked his interrogator

whether he thought birds knew

what ornithologists thought of them

I had that in mind when I looked through my binoculars

at almost invisible birds wrought large

suddenly

brightly colored

greens

yellows

rust reds

and wondered what type of birds they were

why should I care

I asked myself

the birds themselves don't know

this year my sister and brother in-law

Beth and Larry

pulled off

what even for them

was an amazing feat of hosting celebrations

first it was Avishai's bar-mitzvah

then Pesach

and finally

Sheva and Reuven's wedding

As I watched them

in their natural habitat

move

apparently effortlessly

from one pregnant moment

to another

I struggled to find a category

that would help me understand what was

happening

what was I witnessing

and then I gave up

and just let it be

becoming one of the birds

and leaving ornithology for the

wannabees

In a Road Trip State of Mind

I don't know why

but I am always surprised

when I remember

that insects make beautiful music

some mornings I stop to

listen to the song of a

cardinal couple

who live on our block

I've even had a chance to

watch them flitter

from tree to fence

in our back yard

a fine looking pair

striking in color

magnificent in flight

last year at Tyler's

bar-mitvah

we walked to shul

along a spring

of cold bubbling water

that rushed down the mountain

through the city

and alongside the chapel

with a sound that was an

ovation to the grand

and sharp splendor

of its surroundings

just a week or two ago

Tzippy and I were

sitting outside

when we heard the

staccato beat of woodpeckers

echoing

riding a wave of breeze

that also carried with it

the rich sweetness of honeysuckle

and somehow

insects

which can never be said

to be beautiful ....

last year

after a full day of activity

and a campfire dinner

A.Y., Tzippy and I

fell into one of those

glorious

camping sleeps

serenaded by a

symphony of sound

more splendid than

any composed by man

at the very least

a pleasant reminder

of the vital energy

available

to even the humblest amongst us

(speaking of insects

did you ever wonder

how the fly got its name

I mean

there are so many creatures that fly

birds

squirells

even fish

and yet the fly somehow scored the name

fly?)

Crows in the Morning

A murder of crows cawed

closely contiguous

to the covered catacombs

of Coon's Deep Water Lake Campground

they palled around

while the night time chill valiantly held on

and the sun rose above the tree line

Starbux sniffed and demanded to be scratched

the coffee maker gurgled and sputtered

Zaide played solitaire

with real cards on the picnic table

Temimah slept

hoody over head

on her arms

at a picnic table

one over

recovering

after several hours tending to Avishai and Yedida

who tried out for the rodeo

a woodpecker pecked while crickets sang and mosquitos...

oh those dreadful diminutive vampires

how they feasted on our exceptional Karbrinsky blood

demonstrating particular fondness for the light sweet crude
of Shua and Yonah

for some reason ignoring Zaide and Bubby

the Patriarch and Matriarch

entirely

(don't think they weren't hurt by the lack of attention

afforded their septuagenarian veins.)

curls of smoke occasionally rose from the ash filled fire pit

in that very spot

the night before

Moishe tended fire speckled logs

configuring and reconfiguring

the teepee

which formed the core of a nightly schmooze circle.

earlier he had fished off of the pier

casting left handed

his lure-led line arcing and then landing

with that gorgeous sound made by lures on glassy lake
surfaces the world over

as the sun set

painting the mirror image of the oak

pine

and maple

the blue sky and wisps of clouds

Chananya slept

exhausted

from whistle-lisping subtle innuendo to Starbux

Appendix I

The Rodeph Shalom's (Pursuer of Peace) Manifesto

Sometimes, right before I fall asleep, I imagine that I won the lottery. I pick an amount, the number keeps on getting bigger, lately it has been two hundred million dollars (a hundred million just doesn't do it for me any more); and I imagine what I would do with it. I've decided I would take it up front, in a lump sum, and after taxes that might be ... I want family members to get a lot, I want to give a lot to Tzedaka. Then there are the investments, a house, cars... and ... zzzzzzzzzzzzzzzzzzzzzzzzz.

I have asked myself, more than once, why I choose to imagine these unlikely scenarios, when I could just as easily spend a few minutes thinking about how I could make my life better, I mean really better. Or perhaps, I've asked myself; "could I spend a minute or two thinking about how I could make someone else's life better? Now wait, don't do that thing with your eyes, he's getting all preachy; this is going to be boring, thing. Give me a minute to convince you that this is something you want to pay attention to. This is something that will not only enhance your life; this is something that will change the world as we know it, for the better.

If you are like most people you are frustrated. You are hurting; after all people can be crummy. Just look around you. All people you know have someone they hate and someone who hates them. People don't trust each other. We have to lock everything. There are so many walking wounded; wounded by people who said hurtful things at crucial moments that continue to reverberate in the heads of others for an eternity. Look at how much energy is spent hating or recovering from hate. Imagine what we could do with all of that energy.

As Jews we are told that our present situation is a result of a particularly pernicious period of hatred that resulted in the destruction of the Second Bait Hamikdosh; and from the looks of things, we haven't fixed the problem. Have you ever tried to imagine what it would take to make things right? To have a healthy, productive, people who would take creation forward; to have a relationship with Hashem that was open and vibrant; to have all of our national institutions back in operation, humming along towards goodness. You may have tried to imagine this, but you probably didn't get very far. How could you, where would you find the strength to imagine it? Why can't someone come up with a creative solution, you wonder, to end the violence directed at Israel or for that matter, the violence perpetrated by other anti-Semites throughout the world. After all, we are a people celebrated for our creative intellect, and here we are, not only reviled by many, but mired in our own mutual dislike. And our only resolutions for this problem of consuming hatreds are actions that would have had us sent to the corner in first grade.

You're reading this thinking, I don't have the time or energy to solve global problems, I can barely get through the day. I have family issues, community issues, things happening at work.

Honestly, I wish I could care enough about the global stuff, I just can't. I don't have the energy.

That's where I come in. I'm going to help. Of course I can only help, you've got to follow through. But when you do, the topography of your life will change. You will experience quiet, renewed vigor and expansive joy.

Several years ago a collection of Jewish people from Chicago and the suburbs got together to deal with hatred amongst Jews. They formed two groups. They called them One Groups. The purpose of these groups was to help its members develop doable, individual, projects that would heal rifts and build bridges. The first meetings were charged with energy. There were people representing many strata of Jewish society that rarely interact with each other. There were Kach members and liberal Jews, there were Lubavitchers and Litvaks, and there were conservative Jews and modern orthodox Jews and so on. Take a minute and try to imagine the scene. Norman Rockwell should have been there to paint it. There were awkward moments as members found ways to interact with each other, but everyone who was there was dedicated to making it work and found ways to make that happen. It was decided early on that the meetings would not be places for mere venting or catharsis; they would not be support groups, but think tanks. People would suggest projects, and they would be hashed out. If there was a problem, someone would identify it and then come up with a solution; and then the individual would go off to perform it. At the next meeting, the group would listen to the result and comment. The purpose was to inspire, to encourage the project, and provide motivation for the person to follow through. Much of the motivation was the knowledge that he or she would have to face their peers at the next meeting, all of whom were anxious to hear the results. Remember these were designed to be doable. They were small steps. It didn't matter how big the project was as long as something was being done. Some people discovered they could do a lot more than they thought. Others discovered that what they thought was doable was more difficult than they imagined. This information was then used when designing the next project.

The groups lasted about a year and then disbanded. It was hard to keep the fire of the first meetings alive from month to month (they met once a month). But a formula was distilled from the creative thinking of the group. In fact, I've written a news release that sums it up well. Here it is:

CHICAGO-August 26th, 2008, the Norwegian Nobel Committee announced that it will reveal the winner of the Nobel Peace Prize on October 11. Missing from the list of those nominated is the One Project, but if its members have their way, in a few years there will be no need for a Peace Prize.

"We have crafted a solution to strife and hatred in the world. No more hoping that one day there will be peace, now we can make peace happen," Yehoshua Karsh, a member of the One Project, said on Wednesday.

Project One, a grass roots organization founded by members of the Jewish community in Chicago devoted to healing rifts and building bridges within the Jewish community, announced on Wednesday that they have distilled a "peace formula," that is ready for immediate use.

"It is simple, it is elegant, and the minute you hear it, you know it will work. We studied different models and identified what was working and what wasn't. After some tinkering we developed our formula, we tested it and it works," said Karsh.

"The formula is: "Heal a rift, build a bridge." There are just two steps to implementing it: 1. Pick a small project. Make up with your spouse, child, parent, friend, colleague, synagogue member, etc. If you have hard feelings towards others, call them, send them a card, some flowers, an e-mail; hug them, and say you're sorry. It doesn't matter if you were right. Be humble and give in. Do it immediately, don't wait. 2. Think of someone who is alone, feels ostracized, harassed, or disenfranchised. Call this person and invite him or her to dinner or send them a card or e-mail just to say hi. Do it immediately, don't wait."

"The beauty of this is, you don't have to rely on anyone else to solve the problem. You don't have to go somewhere to make things better. You don't have to tackle a project you can't handle. This is like aspirin. After the development of aspirin, if someone called a doctor and complained of a headache, the doctor said, "Take two aspirin and call me in the morning." Now if someone calls you, feeling crummy and hopeless because of all of the strife and hatred in the world; you can tell them, "Do these two things and call me in the morning."

You are not going to wait to begin; you are going to make it happen now. Just like it said in the news release, you will concentrate on two modes of action. Healing rifts and building bridges. These will be small very doable projects. Your first area of concentration will be on healing the rifts that are closest to you and the easiest to heal. If you had a spat with your spouse, sibling, parent, child, a friend, neighbor, colleague, or a member of your shul, and it's still fresh, not yet hardened, that's a good place to start. Call, e-mail, visit, and tell him or her you are sorry.

Don't explain your behavior; just say you are sorry for any pain that you caused. It doesn't matter if you think you were right. You might think that there was some important principle involved. That's probably your anger talking. When you're angry, you can't think straight; but after a while you'll see that the principle was not so important. And even if it was an important principle, you probably didn't have to end up with hard feelings. You could have been creative, thoughtful, sensitive, and found a way to make your point without the hard feelings. And let's say it was one of those extremely rare cases where there was no other way to make your point, apologize anyway. There is something much bigger than your principle at stake here, getting out of the quagmire we find ourselves in. We're in quicksand and the first step to our escape is to stop the struggle. We've got to diffuse the hate. So suck in your gut and apologize.

Next is bridge building; you're going to look around you and find someone who you think might feel disenfranchised, people who don't feel that he or she fit in. It could be because they are new to your community, or because people consider them different or strange. They might not have family or friends. It could be they are alone because they've done things that others are upset about. It doesn't matter what the reason is; the point is they are alone. You need to build a bridge. Again our focus is small doable steps. Maybe you just need to smile when you see them, or say hello, or ask them what their name's are. If you can, invite them over for Shabbos or a Shabbos meal, or just a meal during the week. If they are single you might think of a shidduch for them or introduce them to a shadchan. Suggest they attend a class that you think would be good for them. If you're feeling bold, you might think in terms of a group and not just a person. There might be groups of people who feel disenfranchised; teenagers who are at risk, a political group with extreme positions. You might reach out to them. Talk; invite them to meet your friends, etc. The purpose is not to change each other's positions, but to create lines of communication, of warmth and friendship. If you have family members that you've never really had much contact with, or an old friend you fell out of touch with, this is the best place to start. You will not only be helping another person, you will be enriching your own life.

This project requires three steps: The first is what I am going to identify as our "Klal Gadol." This is the principle that will direct our entire behavior:

Whatever and whomever I come in contact with will be better off for having come in contact with me.

If you had only one rule of thumb and that was it, you couldn't help but be a Tzadik. In order for you to pull that off, you are going to have to know how to make another person better off. You might assume that you know that intuitively. This is often not the case. In order to know what to do, you are going to need steps two and three.

Step two is paying attention to the person who is the object of your focus. You listen and watch and care about him or her. You might assume that you are always doing that. That is unlikely. Paying attention is one of the great challenges for human beings. It is actually a skill that is developed after many frustrating attempts. Every once in a while you just ask yourself, what can I do to make that person's life better. You'd be surprised what you can discover with just a little effort.

The third step is that you are going to love this person. You might think you must love the person before you ever get started, and that is best; but it isn't necessary. You can start by giving and the giving itself generates love, which then fuels the process. At first you do it because you know it's the right thing to do. This is fueled by your intellect and the pain involved in the alternative. Once you've started the giving, the love kicks in and then you won't need the good intentions. You'll give because you need to give to someone you love.

One of the lessons you will learn early on is that you have not necessarily improved someone's life just by introducing something new to it. We assume that when we've identified a problem mixed into the person's life and switched things around, our job is over. That is rarely the case. You want to know that you've succeeded in building that bridge or healing that rift, that what you've done will have legs and eventually stand on its own. You must continue to pay attention, see if what you did actually works. If not, you will have to adjust, tinker, meddle some more. You may have to approach a mentor or read a book devoted to this, something that will teach you something you don't already know. Then you are going to have to apply it and pay attention to how it is working.

A wise man once told me that it takes a wise person to make peace. You must become that wise person.

I know that this doesn't sound exciting. There won't be the adrenaline rush of starting a new organization, of challenging the status quo. There won't be rallies, press conferences, or lapel buttons. Charismatic, famous, people won't announce that they are joining your project. This is just you, doing apparently mundane acts of goodness. But this will work, and the other stuff never has. Just make the effort once and I guarantee that you will feel that this is right. And as for the big picture, you just have to open a pin hole and Hashem will take it from there.

Appendix II

Davening on Hot Coals
(Tefillah Like You Mean It)

I want to thank my mentors and colleagues who took time to look over earlier versions of this essay. Their many comments and suggestions are apparent in the final draft. They are Rabbi Michel Twerski, Rabbi Dr. Akiva Tatz, Rabbi Mordechai Becher, Rabbi Dr. Nathan Lopes Cardozo, Rabbi Avraham Edelstein. I also want to than Rabbi Menachem Nissel for his painfully direct and meaningful criticism, and for devoting more time than he had to for this. Thanks to Jacob Brudoley for suggesting that I write the original essay and to Jacob and Sherri for providing initial funding for its production. Thank you to Sheldon Mazor, Janet Cohen, and Alysa Hoffman for their thoughts and comments. Thank you to Rivka Lev for her very professional proofreading of the original manuscript. Thank you to Rabbi Pinchas Langer for hiring me to teach Tefillah at Shayara. It was there that much of the material in the essay was developed. Thank you to Miriam Shreiber, publisher of Jewish Image magazine, for publishing much of my writing and for publishing an early version of this essay. I would like to thank Jemsem.org, Jerusalem Seminary Connection, for sending this essay to their subscribers for criticism and comment. I would like to thank my mother and my father for many things and specifically for editing this essay. Thank you to Hashem Yisborach.

Chapter One

Twenty years ago I began teaching the ideas that make up this book. My purpose then was to help my students experience meaningful tefillah and not just understand the words or the history behind it. I once polled a class of mine, asking the students to raise their hands if they had ever studied tefillah before. They all raised their hands. Then I asked if they had enjoyed the study, and many hands were lowered. I learned, over time, that first people had to experience meaningful davening, and only then would they have the drive to go deeper.

Imagine for a moment that you are a teenager, and at every family gathering your mother tells you to go over to your Uncle Leo and say hello to him. Your Uncle Leo is in his eighties, doesn't talk much, and is the last person on earth you would like to make conversation with. But, to please your mother, you end up going over to say hello to him; and whenever you do, he smiles, asks you how you are; then follows an awkward silence.

Then one day your parents sit you down and explain the facts of your family finances. You have never lacked for anything in your short life, but that was not because your parents were wealthy. It was because Uncle Leo never married and never had children. When you were born, he told your parents that whatever you wanted, he would pay for. You went to private school, you went to summer camp, and you had all of the most up to date clothing and electronics all because of the generosity of Uncle Leo. You can be certain that the next time you see Uncle Leo, things will be different. You will no longer need to be told to go over and say hello, you will do it on your own; and during those awkward silences, you will be the one to make conversation. You will want to know every detail about this man, whom you have now, come to love.

This became my model for teaching tefillah, first help the students experience a connection with the Divine, the sublime joy and awakening of love that comes with making intimate contact, and the gratitude that comes of receiving. And only then, teach the hows, the whys, and the history of davening.

One of my personal rules when teaching this subject is to teach only things I, myself, have experienced. This is important for two reasons: First, if the goal of my teaching is to actually pass on meaningful practices, I had to know that they were in fact meaningful. Even more importantly I know that my students will learn from what I do, not necessarily from what I say. It is in keeping with that rule that the tone of this book is candid, forthright and simple. This is not a scholarly work; it is a practical guide to meaningful davening, based on my own experience.

What are my qualifications for writing this? I rarely looked forward to davening. In fact, I often dreaded it. It was a source of secret embarrassment and shame. There, I said it. I feel like I'm standing up at a "Never liked Davening Anonymous" meeting.

My early experience with tefillah was sort of like "The Emperor's New Clothes." I looked around at my friends and teachers davening and assumed they were all blissfully engaged, that I was the only one whose mind was wandering. I couldn't tell anybody about it or get any tips on how to make things better because if they found out that I was spending my time daydreaming, I would be the laughing stock of the school. I do remember asking one of my teachers how he managed to daven with kavannah. I must have been in eighth grade, and I remember him telling me it wasn't easy for him. His expression made it clear that it was an issue he thought about often. It took me a long time to realize that if I was in a room with a lot of people davening, very few of them were actually concentrating on their davening. I'm not saying this to judge others, just to put the problem in perspective.

What is the problem? For the sake of clarity I've chosen two issues to focus upon. The first is the feeling that I'm actually doing something important. I know that if I really experienced davening that made a difference, I would do it with gusto. The second is paying attention. We're supposed to pay attention to what we're saying, but I found that I couldn't focus for more than a few seconds without my mind wandering.

I hope you're ready for change. Because once you apply the ideas in this book, your life will not be the same. Hashem is going to be front and center, and the texture of your days will be vivid and full of color. At the same time, you will discover that davening happens in the context of a relationship. When it comes to relationships, you have to be willing to take chances. You have to be open to the possibility that you'll be hurt or disappointed. If you insist on always playing it safe, what you end up with will be static and unsatisfying.

Chapter Two

Over the years I've asked many groups of people to raise their hands if they thought Hashem loved them; only a few have. While the few hands were still raised I asked if they thought Hashem liked them, (and even some of those were lowered.) What if you think Hashem doesn't like you? What if you think He hates you? How can you expect to find davening meaningful? How can you be motivated to improve the experience when the end result will be spending intimate time with a Being who hates you?

It is axiomatic that Hashem loves, us, that he treasures us. And it's not just theology; it's our everyday experience. You experience a benevolent order in every aspect of your life. It is what allows you to make plans, to drive amidst other drivers, to send your children on an airplane, and the like. There is not, as a rule, randomness in your life. It is true that sometimes unexplained phenomena occur. They can be painful, evil, terrible, but they are only that when compared to the norm. You are confused by painful events only because they stand in stark contrast to the general experience of your life. Your life is continuously moved by an Order in the Universe, and that Order is primarily benevolent. You don't simply know about it, you rely upon it.

How many things had to go right for you to have a great day? Hundreds, maybe thousands of good things had to happen.

The water pressure in the shower was good, the water was hot, the sun was shining, and so on. How many things must go wrong for you to have a crummy day, two, maybe three? If four major things went wrong you would be on the News. Your everyday experience of the Order of the Universe is that it is primarily benevolent; and yet for many of us, that is not what we see.

One of the main culprits in this deception is low self-esteem. Chances are, if you don't like yourself, your world looks pretty bleak. We tend to project what we are feeling on a screen, which is the world around us. If you don't feel good on the inside, the world doesn't look good on the outside. And if you aren't feeling good about yourself, you are going to assume that Hashem doesn't like you either.

If this is how you're thinking, don't give up. You can change how you feel about yourself; and as you do, your assumptions about how He feels will change as well. Davening can actually help make that happen, but you have to give Hashem some space to show you His love. You have to let Him show you how much He cares for you, how much He does for you.

Maybe you're afraid of the intimacy implied in a relationship with Hashem. You fear you won't have a life. You will have to give up things you enjoy but think G-d won't approve of. And what if you open up and give yourself over to the relationship, and He doesn't respond in kind? The bottom line is, you aren't asking Him to get involved in your life; He already is. You're just opening your eyes to the fact that He's there, that He's involved in all of the details of what you're doing; and when your relationship with G-d gets deeper, your life will become more meaningful. You will discover that you enjoy more, not less; and that what you really need, Hashem alone can provide. The other stuff was just that – stuff. Yes, it's true that sometimes a close relationship with Hashem can leave you vulnerable to more pain; but along with that risk, comes the certainty that your life will be more purposeful.

We are going to be focusing on that aspect of tefillah that is "supplication." We are going to be asking for things. There are also "thank yous," and "praises," and tefillos that teach us what we should strive for. However, we've got to begin at the beginning, and the beginning is asking for things. The love of a child for his parent is founded on the gratitude he has for what he has received. The first thought in all loving relationships is: "What will I get out of this?" As we mature there is sharing, and when we've really matured, each side gives, many times no longer concerned about receiving. A relationship with Hashem is no different. First we need to experience receiving and develop gratitude. Once we've practiced asking for things, then we can apply our experience to the other more sophisticated aspects of tefillah, which are more about giving and sharing.

Chapter Three

I'm going to introduce to you two techniques I've been using. They all involve practice, but they show results immediately.

The first technique is simply to ask Hashem for something. Not only will you ask Him for something, you will get it – whatever you want. Yes, you read that correctly, whatever you want. He's ready to do this at any moment; you just have to ask.

"I've done that zillions of times and I hardly ever get what I asked for," you say, incredulously. You might think you asked Hashem for things, but did you really? Did you ask like someone who really believed he was going to get what he requested, or like someone who, if he received it, would feel like he won the lottery? Imagine going to your boss and asking him for a raise the way you ask Hashem for things, with no feeling and no expectation of receiving it. Do you think for a minute that you would get that raise?

Also, much of the time we ask Hashem for things we don't really even want. What I mean by that is, we think we want these things; but if we were really honest with ourselves, we would realize that we don't want them that much. For instance: if, when I ask Hashem to end the suffering in the Sudan, I measured the intensity of my feeling with some kind of an intensity detector; on a scale of one to ten, my tefillah might register a four. If I asked for tickets to a sold-out ball game or some very popular, state of the art, electronic device, it would measure off the scale. The problem is that I don't ask for the tickets because I think it's petty, and I ask for the end of starvation, but I don't feel strongly about it. So my experience with davening is that I ask for things that I really don't care that much about, never really expecting to get what I ask for. I'm embarrassed by the reality of my wishes and desires and therefore live in yawn-filled denial.

This is now going to change because we're going to ask for things that we really, really, want. We're going to expect to get them; and finally, we're going to get them. When we've done this a few times, our relationship with Hashem will change forever. Our lives will change forever.

This is what you do. Find something that you want. It can be something small, like tickets to something, or it can be big like a shiddach, or the healing of a loved one. All that matters is that you really want it. I mean *really* want it, so intensely that you feel the need burning in your gut.

Step two: you must believe that Hashem will give this to you. He certainly can give it to you. He can do anything. He loves you, and He wants you to be happy.

I know that you're thinking: "What if it's something He doesn't want me to have?" First of all, who do you think gets you those things? Do you think you're getting them on your own? He's getting those things for you anyway. Secondly, we aren't doing this just to get things. This isn't about things; this is about a relationship with Hashem. This is just the way we're going about making it happen. Again, think of the bond of a child to his parent. It begins with the child asking (demanding, really) and receiving what he asked for. That is the basis of what later becomes a love defined by and founded upon gratitude. Sure, we should want more sophistication than that. We shouldn't have to get new things in order to have gratitude. We should be able to feel as profoundly about other people's needs as we do about our own. But the reality is, most of us don't. And if we wait until we do, we'll be waiting forever.

There are some of you who are wondering, what if the answer is no? What if I want something, and He is determined that I shouldn't get it? I have guided many people, including my sons, in what I'm suggesting you do. The experience has always been deep and meaningful. No one I know has regretted embarking on this journey. Be wary of getting too philosophical when you daven. There's a time for tefillah and a time for learning; when you daven, you have to be focused and motivated; your tefillos need to be simple and meaningful. If you start dissecting them as they emerge, you interrupt the flow and stifle the passion of your expression. Leave the philosophy for later. I assure you, that when you work through your experience later on, you will come to the conclusion that your tefillos were answered. While you are davening, be assured of that, and let it flow. And don't hesitate to ask for something huge. If you have a child who is ill, ask Hashem to heal him. He is the source of healing; the doctor is simply the conduit. Don't hold back.

A common piece of advice that many will offer you is to be careful with what you ask for because you might get it and then regret it. This is a self-defeating thought for you at this stage. Yes, it is possible that what you ask for might not be good for you, but never asking for anything would be much worse for you. You must take some risks. And why are you certain that you're so out of touch with yourself that you can't be trusted to ask for what you want? You must go for it.

So, here's what you're going to do: **You're going to find something that you really want. And you're going to ask Hashem for it, once a day.** The best time for this is at the end of the Shmoneh Esreh, before you take your three steps back. A wise man told me that if you insert your tefillah there, the Shmoneh Esreh fuels the tefillah and gives it power. Of course, you don't have to do it then, you can ask for it any time you want and wherever you are. Be sure to ask for it in your own language, in a way that expresses your feelings most honestly.

Hashem's response is immediate. It just takes time for us to see that. I suggest you keep a diary for the next week or two. Write down anything that seems related to what you asked for. If you asked for tickets to the Super Bowl and a friend called to tell you he knows someone who has tickets, write that down, along with any other related phenomena. If you're davening for a shiddach and someone calls you with an idea, write that down. You'll see an immediate increase in activity, and shortly you will receive the answer to your tefillos.

Remember, you aren't doing this to test Hashem; you're just paying attention to something that is going on all of the time.

When you start seeing all of the activity in response to your tefillos, it can be scary. You may get so frightened that you want the whole thing to stop. Don't! Just pull yourself together and let it happen. The fear is momentary and passes quickly. When it happens, write that down too, so that later on, when you need a boost of faith, you can look back at it.

Warning: talking about your results with too many people takes away from the effect. When your tefillos are answered, you're so excited that you want to tell everybody. There's nothing wrong with doing that, but when you talk about things that have the potential to affect you, it diminishes their power. Just as it is therapeutic to talk about things that hurt you because talking about your issues lessens their impact, so too talking about something sweet and wondrous can also lessen its impact. So maybe the first time you'll tell everybody about the results of your tefillos; but you'll see what I mean, and then the next time, you'll start paying attention just for the sake of the relationship and keep it quieter. Keep on doing this. Ask for things, watch them for a while, keep a journal, get them, and then ask for some other things until you've built up a reserve of experience. Once you feel you have a good reserve, you can slowly move to the next level and incorporate some of the more sophisticated techniques mentioned in the Gemara or other seforim.

Now, after all of that, some of you are wondering, what does that have to do with tefillah? Well, my friend, that was tefillah. The best metaphor I can find to explain the difference between what we just talked about and what you find in a siddur, is the difference between a musical novice playing a simple song and a professional musician playing a symphony. The tefillos were written by nevi'im and chachomim and were exquisitely composed. If you sat at a piano and played something like chopsticks, you played music. It wasn't Beethoven, but it was music. You will never play Beethoven if you don't first play something like chopsticks. Someday, with practice, you'll be able to daven with the sophistication that is available in the composed tefillos; but first, you have to cut your teeth on the core of tefillah. And believe me, when you practice asking Hashem for things, you will see an immediate improvement in the intensity you experience during the composed tefillos.

Chapter Four

We are now moving from a technique that brings a sense of meaning to your tefillos, to one that will help you focus, and stay focused on them. And while the previous section deals with teffilah that can be done outside of the formal structure of composed tefillah, the following technique is specifically designed to enhance your experience during formal dovening. This technique involves relaxation and full breathing, both before and during your davening. Some people call this "meditation;" I call it "paying attention." The minute you mention "meditation" or "breathing" to people, they get apprehensive; it sounds strange, and mysterious. It isn't. It is simply applying techniques you have done many times; you just didn't call it meditation.

In the past when you read something interesting and realized only an hour later that your leg fell asleep, you were meditating. Women who practice Lamaze use it when they deliver their babies. People who suffer anxiety use it to relax. Some people call it self-hypnosis and use it to deal with pain or to remember lost moments. You're going to use it because with a little practice, you'll be able to deeply concentrate on anything you want to, for a significant period of time.

Tool #1

Breathing

The key to this process is taking relaxed, full, breaths. Exhale all of the air from your lungs (without straining), pause for a moment, and then fill your lungs completely. Exhale again and remove all of the air from your lungs. Remember not to strain; empty them the best you can. Pause for a moment and then fill your lungs again. Don't pause after you inhale. Once you fill your lungs, begin to exhale. Don't rush. Breathe fully and comfortably.

After just a few moments you will be more relaxed, alert, and focused. The longer you keep up your breathing, the deeper and more pronounced, the effect.

Tool #2

Relaxing your body

This is best done sitting comfortably, but can also be done standing. Close your eyes and silently ask your body to relax. Imagine waves of relaxation rippling from your head to your toes. Focus on your toes and relax them; they might tingle as they relax. Next, your feet; focus on them and they will relax as well. Move step by step through your body, relaxing each part as you come to it. Pay special attention to your stomach area, your back, your shoulders, your neck, your face, and your forehead. These muscles gather tension and often require more attention before they fully relax.

If your mind wanders, gently bring it back to relaxation. Don't worry if it wanders. Don't struggle to focus. When you notice it wandering, acknowledge what you're thinking about, go back to where you wandered from and continue.

Eventually you'll develop your own breathing and relaxation techniques. There aren't any fixed rules when it comes to breathing and relaxing; do whatever works for you.

Chapter Five

Three Scenarios

Scenario #1

You have five to ten minutes to spend in a quiet place before davening.

Scenario #2

You have a moment to spend before davening.

Scenario #3

You are in the middle of the Shmoneh Esreh and you discover that your mind has just traveled elsewhere.

Scenario number one is the best-case scenario. Five to ten minutes is enough time to relax and focus your thoughts. In this case, you begin with your breathing and combine it with relaxation. Once you're relaxed, you can just focus on your breathing. When your mind wanders, gently bring it back to your breathing. You can also choose to follow your thoughts and let them go wherever they want; you are simply an observer taking note of your thoughts. You can also use that time to introduce a specific thought or visualization that will prepare you for tefillah. Rebbitzen Feige Twerski once suggested a visualization to a class of mine and I've used it many times. Just before Shemoneh Esreh, after you've taken your three steps back, you picture yourself standing in front of huge wooden doors. They slowly open before you; and from inside, someone, using your full Hebrew name, announces that you are ready for an audience with their father, the King. You then take your three steps forward, through the doors for your audience with the King. I can't describe how powerful that is.

Scenario number two is the most common; you have just a moment before davening. In this case, start some deep breaths and generally relax yourself. Ten deep breathing cycles will greatly enhance your focus. If you still have time for visualization like the one mentioned above, go for it. If you find your mind wandering later in the davening, pause and do some more deep breathing; you should easily regain your focus.

Scenario number three is embarrassingly common. You find yourself in the middle of Shmoneh Esreh, and you're not even sure how you got there. Stop for a moment and begin your deep breathing. Do at least three cycles and try to generally relax; for the next while, daven with your breathing. You do this by saying the words during the exhalations and remaining silent while you inhale. You might need to pause in between brachos for more breathing and relaxing. During that time, you can focus on the general meaning of the next brachah. Remember, when your mind does wander, don't strain; take note of the fact that your mind wandered and then gently return to breathing and relaxing and the simple meaning of the words.

If you follow the steps outlined above, you're guaranteed to experience profound clarity in your tefillah, but not every day. In practice you will discover that you never have the same experience twice; and yes, there are some days when it's a struggle to focus on anything. Don't let those days discourage you. Keep at it, and you will experience tefillah as you always dreamed you would.

So that's it, short and sweet. Don't wait to implement these steps, do them now. I can't tell you how important these have been to me. There is nothing more important to me than my relationship with Hashem, and these simple tools took that relationship to undreamed of heights.

LaVergne, TN USA
23 August 2009
155692LV00001BA/4/P